West Side Girl

Anita Solick Oswald

TABLE OF CONTENTS

Liberty and Justice for All

Dedication

Thanks to the following individuals who helped me bring the West Side Girl stories to life:

Ralph Oswald, for your patience, reading, re-reading, and editing my tales

Barbara and Deirdre O'Loughlin, for encouraging me to write the stories I entertained you with when you were growing up

Barbara Ryan and Donna Cristo, for filling in the details of our shared childhood

Nicole Bouchard, for your encouragement and for gently editing my manuscript

Robert Gatewood and the Boulder Writing Studio for providing a nurturing environment to develop my manuscript and for cheering me on

St. Mel-Holy Ghost School alumni and staff and West Side former residents, for being an important part of my childhood, reading my stories, and sharing your memories

These stories are dedicated to:

Declan Delaney Stoddard, the best grandson in the world, because I love you.

Helen and Jack Solick, my parents, and Helen and Bill McMahon, my grandparents, and all my relatives for giving me a golden childhood. You are always with me.

Introduction

I have a recurring dream that I'm back on Madison Street. I walk west from the Marbro Theater to my old home. Every building holds a memory for me—Madigan Brothers, where my Mom shopped for our holiday outfits, Red Goose shoes, where I x-rayed my feet under the fluoroscope, Ebert's Studio, where my parents had my baby pictures taken, Pendola's drugstore and soda fountain, where my Mom first heard the news that Pearl Harbor had been bombed. In my dream, the neighborhood is renewed and the street is busy with shoppers and traffic. Nostalgically, I stop by my old home, investors have purchased the building. They have restored the restaurant to its original beauty and replaced the stained glass windows. It is open for business. I talk to the owners about my family and about the years they operated the restaurant. I think they have done a beautiful job restoring the restaurant.

I go upstairs to the apartment where I grew up. The investors are turning the apartments into condos. They give me a tour. The empty rooms remind me of the day we moved from Madison Street and never returned. The fixtures and wood cabinets are long gone, but the wood floors have been refinished and the large bathroom is remodeled. I remember birthdays, anniversaries, Christmas, childhood illnesses, and parties—everything important in my first fourteen years was associated with this apartment. I am happy that my old home has been renovated in such a loving way. I wish I could move back there. I want to buy one of the condos and I think of asking my sisters to buy in with me.

I wake up from my dream. Urban renewal never came to West Madison Street.

My parents, brother, and grandparents are gone, as are my cousins, aunts, and uncles.

I remember the Google satellite picture and the trash filled vacant lots and the ghost town I saw so vividly, and I feel sad and empty. Instead of my dream shoppers, the streets are empty except for a few men standing on the corner and the store advertisements are covered in graffiti. The old high school and convent are gone. Our beautiful home on Madison Street is an empty lot and it looks so small.

All I have left are the memories of a family. Generations of Solicks, who worked, lived, loved, married, and raised families at this address in this neighborhood. I want to erect a plaque to all of them.

I lived on Madison Street in 4200 block during the 1950s and 1960s. The Madison-Crawford area was a busy commercial district on the West Side of Chicago. My parents made their home in an apartment on the third story over the Bohemian restaurant where my great grandfather built a grocery and butcher store. My dad's entire family worked in the restaurant at one time or another. We looked down on a fabulous flashing neon sign complete with dancing Christmas trees and the family name—Solick's—in lights. It made us feel like players in a romantic, glamorous world.

As children, we saw only the beauty and could not see the threadbare edges of our neighborhood. While there were still lots of businesses: a department store, drug stores, grocers, candy stores and three movies theaters within a block of our house, the West Side, which had seen its heyday in the twenties, was on the way down. After World War II, the housing shortage resulted in many two and three flats being broken up into rooms for rent. At that point, it was not uncommon for basements, damp and barely suitable as living quarters, to be rented to immigrants from all over.

The parish was the center of the neighborhood's spiritual, social, and academic lives. I attended St. Mel-Holy Ghost School, the same school our parents attended. I was baptized at the same church where my parents were married, the church that my grandparents, great-grandparents, aunts, and uncles built. The clergy and the nuns ministered to the community, regardless of their religion, and held the community together.

It was a time of great social change and migrations from the South—families from Appalachia where the mines had played out and upwardly mobile blacks seeking housing and good paying factory jobs in the cities. If you know someone who worked in the factory, they could get you in. Immigrants moved west on Madison Street like the early pioneers in search of their fortune, trying to stay one step ahead of the hoards. The "hillbillies" slept in shifts in the rooming houses and apartments until they could afford better housing. The black families sacrificed to send their kids to the parochial school so they could have a better education. We lived in the apartment from the late 1940s until 1963. From Truman to Kennedy, from the early days of television to the *Jetsons*, from McCarthyism to the inception of the civil rights movement.

Because I was an apartment dweller, I combed the residential streets to the north and south of Madison in search of adventure. I often walked with my sisters and brother over to Monroe Street to play or meet kids that did not attend our parochial school. We liked to play baseball in a vacant dirt lot across the alley. Behind the large apartment building there was housing for whites from the south, Puerto Ricans escaping New York, and immigrants from Eastern Europe. Our playmates were second generation Italian, Greek, Puerto Rican, Mexican, Irish, Polish, Romanian, Jewish, Catholic, Protestant, African American, and immigrants. Some did not speak English when they started school. Some did not have a change of clothes. You either attended the parochial school at St. Mel's or the public school, Tilton.

Growing up in an integrated neighborhood is a great leveler. I either liked a kid or I didn't. I wanted to hang out with them or I didn't. I never saw a difference between me and other kids. Blind children and hearing impaired kids, as well as children with other disabilities attended our school. They were our friends. We wore uniforms to school every day and could only tell what grade a girl or boy was in by the color of their scarf or tie. We were all the same.

My parents grew up in the same neighborhood where we lived. Many of our relatives, including my maternal grandparents lived in the neighborhood. Even though the neighborhood was transitional, I had a lot of freedom to play and explore. Our adventures extended to the City of Chicago, since we were only five miles from the Loop. Chicago was my personal playground. I could hop on the bus or the L and make it downtown to visit the museums downtown shops. I just had to be home before dark. My neighborhood was home to beautiful movie theaters, a branch library, and parks. I went to Off the Street Club for after school activities like roller skating. Or I would just hang out at the playground or in the streets and alleys.

The neighborhood died because of neglect, aging infrastructure, and unscrupulous real estate agents who sold both fear and dreams.

Eventually everyone who had come to the neighborhood in search of a better life - the gypsies, Mexicans, Puerto Ricans and "hillbillies" - moved away, still searching, still dreaming.

The Old Grounds,
the Gang and Games Afoot

Mama's Got a Tattoo

Monroe Street was a treasure chest of adventure, friends, and instruction in the ways of the world when we were growing up. A potpourri of apartment buildings, boarding houses, single family residences and gray stones lined the street one block south of Madison. Monroe Street was a microcosm of the neighborhood in flux. And there was a hierarchy. There were house proud long time homeowners who would chase you away from their postage stamp size lawns. There were renters who had been established in the nicer apartments for decades, and felt as entitled as the homeowners; although their living situation was always more tenuous since most of the apartments were month to month rentals. Then there were the newcomers who lived in the tenements, basement apartments, and sleeping rooms. Immigrants from other countries—Russia, Ireland, and Poland—came in a steady stream. Then, came the "hillbillies" in search of good jobs in the Chicago factories. Resented and ridiculed by the old timers, they were followed by Puerto Ricans, Mexicans, and African Americans, called the "colored" or "shines" or worse.

Madison Street was the business district and Barbara and I had the office workers in the Commonwealth Edison building and the denizens of the hotel that rented rooms by the month or the week as our neighbors. We were visitors who dropped in, tolerated by the homeowners. People came and went on busy Madison Street, and they fascinated us from our perch in our third story apartment, but not as much as meeting a new child whose family had come from some other seemingly exotic locale and had moved to our neighborhood on their way up or down, but mostly up.

Running home from our classes at St. Mel's every day, we could not wait to strip off our blue serge uniforms and throw on our play clothes. Then it was out the back door onto the porch and down three flights of wooden stairs, crossing the cobblestone alley that separated us from the home dwellers with real back yards, and running through one of the many gangways in search of fun and new friends. We couldn't run fast enough. Children were moving in and out of the neighborhood during this time; the children came and went with their parents' shabby suitcases and bumpy mattresses. The children trailed along with their parents' jobs and opportunities, and we always needed a fresh supply to keep us entertained.

We headed west toward the vacant lot near the end of the block. Two small girls dug with a stick in the dirt of the small, dry, vacant, and weedy lot where the neighborhood kids held unceremonious games of baseball. The game was on as long as someone had a bat, a ball and a glove. Anyone could join and the rules were very loose. There was no beginning and no end. There was never a winner or loser. The game might still be going on today

Strolling past the lot one day, Mom told us a home once stood on the lot, but had burned to the ground and no one rebuilt on the site. We tried to imagine the house and the family who Mom had known in her childhood, but we could only see the steel drum trash cans that lined the alley to the north. From Monroe Street, you could see all the way through to the alley, and if you were running bases you had to watch out not to trip over the concrete foundation that remained dreaming under the weeds.

The older girl looked up from her artistic pursuits in the dirt as we approached. Like a young Maureen O'Hara, her creamy pale face, large green eyes, and wavy auburn hair spoke of Inishmore and Dun Aengus. Poverty and poor diet had not marred that lovely skin. Dressed in a too short summer frock, she tugged at her waist as she stood up and I saw that she was taller than me. The younger girl stayed crouched in the dirt. She had freckles and startling blue eyes; her front tooth was missing and a new one budded at the gum line. Her faded plaid dress was worn and soiled, a hand-me-down that had seen better days. Her hair was loose, a ribbon still dangling at the end of a lock and her smile made me think of Huck Finn. Both knees were skinned and healing. I knew she would be fun.

I was the first to speak. "Hey, who are you? Whattaya doing? Do you live around here? Where are you from?" The younger girl started to blurt a response but the older sister hushed the younger girl with a squinted eye and a look. "I am Maureen Reilly, don't call me Moe, and this here is my sister, Deirdre." The younger girl chimed in, "Yeah, Deirdre, but you can call me Dee Dee." The girls pointed out the boarding house two doors to the west where they lived with their parents and siblings.

I asked again, "Where are you girls from?" and added, "What school do you go to?"

Maureen looked a bit hesitant, like a cat that is cautious about that first caress from a human. She looked us up and down. But she saw we were just girls, seven and five, and decided to trust us. "Well, we're from here and there. We drove here from Tennessee with some other folks. Daddy got a job at the candy factory." Dee Dee jumped in, "We don't go to no school; we been on the road for a while."

"You don't go to ANY school" I corrected, "but you will—St. Mel's is just a block from here. We all go there." I introduced myself and my younger sister, "I am Anita Solick and this is my sister, Barbara. We live on Madison Street. I am seven and she is five years old." Barb said, "Hi." The Reilly sisters instantly took a liking to Barbara. She was small for her age and looked like a china doll with her dark hair and beautiful blue eyes. I reached my hand out to shake and said, "Do you want to play with us?"

They both grinned and in unison yelled, "Sure!"

Maureen and Dee Dee were our sirens that year. The girls urged us to do things we'd never done before and we were their huckleberries. They had no curfew and were free to roam the neighborhood while their Mom hung out in the gin mill next to the funeral parlor on Madison Street. We had to be in before dark. And when we told our mother where the new girls lived we were forbidden to enter their building. Instead Mom suggested we bring the girls home and they were welcomed. Maureen and Dee Dee had a free pass since they had an Irish last name, even if their parents were "hillbillies". "You stay out of that boarding house they live in, you hear me? That is not a nice place. It probably has bugs."

The Reilly's lived in an apartment on the third floor, but some lower levels had been converted to rooms for rent; and single men, factory workers, newly arrived in the big city, slept in shifts in the rooms to save up money to send home or to get their own place. When we asked why the other floors were rented out by the room, Mom said that there had been a housing shortage after the War, and greedy people divided up the apartments to make a quick profit. Once done, she explained, there was no going back. She mourned the changes on her West Side, the days gone by, and the unusual sleeping arrangements at the Reilly's Monroe address did not seem exotic or interesting to her.

But if Mom said "Don't do it!" the temptation was just that much more tantalizing. Winding our way up the back stairs of the gray stone, Maureen and Dee Dee led us through the netherworld—rooms with shared baths, sleeping rooms that had to be crossed to get to the next sleeping room, rooms that had been converted from a parlor or dining room to a kind of dorm room for men. The venetian shades were always drawn, so we had to wait for our eyes to adjust before we could tiptoe past the occupants, carefully stepping over empty beer bottles. Sparsely furnished, ashtrays overflowing, the rooms smelled of sweaty clothes aired out overnight on a chair and liquor and canned chili heated on a hot plate.

Maureen and Dee Dee stopped to pick a few pennies from a plate on the floor next to a twin bed. The thin man in the bed stirred, snorted and then rolled over and fell back into a deeper sleep. Covered only by a sheet; he slept in his skivvies. His chest and arms were hairy and he needed a shave. A pilly chenille blanket worn through in spots was crumbled on the floor. "It's ok," Maureen explained when I raised my eyebrows, "It's not stealing. He likes us. He told us we could come in and get money for candy any time we wanted. His name is Del and he told us he has two little girls back home just like us." I felt sad for those girls separated from their father. I knew my mother would never approve of our spying at all, and Barb and I made a pact not to mention the sleeping man. We pushed on, snooping around—the lure of the unknown was just too strong.

Barb and I couldn't resist when Maureen and Dee Dee invited us to their apartment, and it felt rude to say no, despite Mom's warnings. Anyway, it was fun. The shabby apartment had almost no furniture, and what furniture the family had was in such poor condition, that the adults did not care if we jumped on it or put our feet on it. In fact, they did not seem to care what we did as long as we were laughing. The living room floor was wood—no rug or carpeting in sight. There were no knickknacks or personal items in sight. The sofa was a sad affair. I'd seen this sofa in so many apartments on Monroe Street. It was standard issue to transient families, but I could not figure out why there were so many of them or why they were made in the first place. I hated the sculpted fake velvet upholstery. Pile as stiff as toothbrush bristles, the arms shone where the upholstery worn off from years of use. Once plump cushions were an uneven landscape now and shiny springs poked through to pinch young thighs. The only caution we received was to be careful and not to lean on the right arm of the sofa; it was broken and the entire side of the sofa would fall off with just a small nudge.

Just as in our home, the kitchen was a hub, and sometimes Maureen, Dee Dee, Barbara and I would sit around the wooden table on the mismatched unpadded chairs while Mrs. Reilly told us stories about growing up in Tennessee. She appeared to be about the same age as my mother, but life had been harder for Mrs. Reilly. Still pretty, if a bit rough around the edges, she opened a bottle of beer, shifted the baby to one knee, lit a cigarette, and patiently answered our questions about growing up in the rural south. "Daddy was a little bit crazy. He was a moonshiner and kind of a hermit, so he wasn't around a whole lot, but he'd stop by with something he killed, like a squirrel or some money from his moonshining. Enough to get us through. My momma raised the seven of us."

Eating squirrel was something I had never imagined possible; I thought you were supposed to feed the rodents peanuts in Garfield

Park, and Mom cautioned us not to get bit or "You'll get rabies." I was also amazed to learn that Mrs. Reilly was a grandmother and that her oldest daughter was eighteen with a child of her own. My grandmother had gray hair and looked like the perfect grandmother that she was. A daughter of eighteen seemed ancient to me; I thought to myself that I would never live to be that old.

"But you look so young," I blurted.

"Well, thank you for that, honey. I was just fourteen when I got married," Mrs. Reilly explained. When I asked why she married when she was just a child, she sighed, "I just got so tired of going to bed hungry."

Her wistful expression told me everything about her interrupted girlhood, the end to her short education, her hard life. Some of my friends had older sisters that were nearly fourteen and they were still kids. I could not imagine caring for a baby when I was fourteen. My mother would certainly not let me care for our baby sister. I was only allowed hold her in my arms while seated on the sofa and only with supervision. I was very curious about the child bride, but, I did not want to hurt Mrs. Reilly's feelings and changed the subject. Anyway, the greatest object of my fascination was on Mrs. Reilly's arm. I bombarded her with questions.

"Will that tattoo wash off? And who is Jimmy? Did it hurt when you got it?"

Mrs. Reilly sported a heart with a Jimmy's name on her left arm. "Oh, that was my first husband," she laughed.

"You had another husband, not Mr. Reilly? Is he dead?"

"I don't think so, honey, he ran off with another gal when I was pregnant with my third child. Haven't seen him since."

She seemed to me to have taken this pretty well, given she'd be stuck with his name on her arm for the rest of her life. "If I had it removed I'd have a nasty scar, and I haven't got up the nerve to do it."

And without being asked, she clarified, "Mr. Reilly is Maureen and Dee Dee's daddy. He found me when I was real low." Her eyes trailed off for a moment, looking back on sad times, and then her expression brightened. "He married me and we had the two girls here and now he brought me here to the big city and this nice home."

We never saw Mr. Reilly, the hero, because he worked the swing shift in the Brach's factory nearby. Like legions of men who moved to Chicago in search of a break, he worked—he worked as much as he could. I guessed he was like our dad, working at some other job on his day off to support his family, and I thought he must be a good man.

The Reilly sisters led us on explorations around Monroe Street. One day we found a small white kitten abandoned in a garbage can. I told the girls I would bring it home and make it our pet. But the cat got a cold reception when I brought it home. Mom did not like cats and we were not allowed to have a pet in the apartment.

"Where'd you get that cat? You found it in a garbage can? Take it back. You'll get ringworm." Teary eyed, I took the kitten back to the alley behind the Reilly girls apartment. They met me there and reassured me.

"That's ok; Mama will let us take care of it. We'll keep her for you."

The kitty grew fat and happy on milk and fatty kitchen scraps from the Reilly kitchen; I'd wave to my kitty friend sunning herself on the third floor back porch every time I passed.

It wasn't a one way friendship because Barb and I had plenty to offer our new friends and we were eager to reciprocate. We had a nice apartment with furniture and toys and lots of treats and candy.

Barb and I always had some money because our Gramps would give us each a dollar on Saturdays when he visited. When we had our combined birthday party, Mom gave gifts to all the party guests. When they showed interest in a toy, I'd pretend I was tired of it and offered it to them. And because our family owned the restaurant, we had access to places the Reilly's did not. Businesses, other restaurants, butcher shops, grocery storerooms.

Gibbons-O'Keefe funeral parlor was a favorite haunt. The proprietor, Tommy Gibbons, was one of my Grandma Lillian's cronies. Walking under the canopy, through the leaded glass doors, to the inner sanctum of the dead, we felt like VIPs. The Reilly girls were in awe. The receptionist or Tommy Gibbons himself would greet us and offer us Tootsie Rolls from a large lead crystal bowl on the desk. Checking out the guestbook to see if anyone we knew was visiting, Mr. Gibbons would tip us off to the fresh funeral arrangements that had been discarded behind the mortuary in the alley. We'd make bouquets and take them home to Mom.

Sometimes we'd stop by the gin mill next door where Mrs. Reilly hung out during the day. The interior of Barnacle Bill's was dark, and the smell of stale beer wafted onto the street. Country music blared from a jukebox in the corner. Barbara and I were not allowed to go in; we would have been consigned to a lifetime of punishment on a dining room chair if Mom caught us anywhere near the place, so we hovered in the doorway while our friends ventured in to get money for a popsicle from their mother. The baby sat staring out into the darkness on Mrs. Reilly's lap. The Reilly girls knew when to time their visits—after Mom had a couple of beers she was more like to part with change. Sometimes the men in the bar would generously chip in. They'd call to us and invite us to join them but we never set a toe on as much as a tile in the entryway. We knew that our mother was omniscient and she would find out eventually.

Our ritual of hooking up with the Reilly girls continued all through the school year. Our quests and escapades took us all over the neighborhood streets and alleys. They showed us new things and we shared our lives. We corrected their spelling and pronunciation and, after a while, they began to sound like Chicago girls. Then, abruptly, in the springtime, life changed. Barbara and I ran home as usual to change and get out to play. The days were getting longer and it was warming up. Mom yelled as I scooted out the door, "Take your sweater!" "It's hot out," I shot back and kept going. But when we got halfway down Monroe Street, we knew something was up.

A beat up old Ford truck was parked outside the Reilly's apartment house. The mattress was lashed to the hood, and the old couch lay in the front yard, up for grabs. A few boxes were in the back filled with pots, pans, nightgowns, diapers, baby bottles—all the Reilly's belongings on display. Maureen and Dee Dee were playing in the lot where we first met them. Mrs. Reilly was seated on the stoop watching the baby, who was walking now, and my cat, was lying next to her while Mrs. Reilly absent mindedly stroked her tummy. I could hear the cat purring.

"Hey—I'm glad you came over so we can say bye." Maureen spoke first. I remembered she'd been the first to greet us.

"Where are you going?" I asked nervously.

"Moving—Daddy got a better job. We've got a new apartment over by the factory and it has a back yard. Do you want your cowgirl doll back?"

"Nah, you can keep it. You know I don't like playing with dolls anyway."

Mrs. Reilly saw my face drop and she chimed in, "Well, maybe you girls can come and visit us. Come give us a hug." She kissed us both on the cheeks and then whispered, "Thanks for being good friends to the girls."

The girls loaded up my cat and climbed in the truck. They waved to us from the back window until they were out of sight. I knew we would never see them again.

Barbara and I tried to make the best of it by continuing our rituals, dropping in at all our old hangouts, but it wasn't nearly as much fun without someone to share it with. It was closing on summer and school would be out soon. Who would we play with? Then, one day after school we saw movement at old Mrs. Leyden's house. Someone was moving in. We had to investigate. I prodded Barbara to hurry up and change and out the back door we tumbled over to Monroe Street. Standing in the middle of the block in front of the ramshackle frame house was a young girl. She looked older than me, maybe ten years old. In fact, she looked like a middle-aged Irish washerwoman. She had shoulder length hair, a fair complexion and thick glasses; her dress was a good one that looked like it had been through the washing machine a thousand times.

I greeted her. "Hi, do you live here now? What's your name?"

With a hint of an English accent, the girl responded, "We're just moving in. My parents bought the house from Mrs. Leyden. My name is Mary Lennon."

Pressing her for more detail, I learned that she had moved from Ireland by way of Liverpool, that her dad had worked on the Canadian railroad and lost his eye in an accident, and that he had moved the family to Chicago and bought a bar and the house with the settlement. This all sounded promising to me.

Then she added, "I have two sisters, Katherine and Patricia, and two brothers, John and James." Barbara and I smiled knowingly at each other—we'd hit pay dirt!

Wild Animals

"Look at those crazy kids—what are they doing?" my Dad exclaimed as he slammed on the brakes. As the buggy (fire chief's car) crossed Keeler and Monroe, westbound past the greystone two flats that lined the street, he saw four tots sprawled on their backs in the middle of Monroe. Another car stopped and the driver cursed and shook his fist at the scamps as he drove around them.

My dad inched the fire chief's car forward, and as he slowly approached, a little tow headed girl, then a small boy, then another girl, and then another very dirty little boy raised their heads. "Son of a bitch! I know those kids!" he shouted. The shock of recognition dawned in the first girl's face. She poked one of the boys and then the two of them jumped up and took off towards the Lennon's gangway. But not fast enough for my dad. He pounced from the buggy to the curb and apprehended his two youngest children—my sister, Donna, and my brother, Jackie.

Marching them through the Lennon's yard, across the alley, and up the stairs, he pounded on the back door of our apartment. My mother was always on the phone. When she finally opened the door, he demanded, "Helen, what the hell are these kids doing lying in the street?" She stared at him uncomprehending and kept talking. He repeated his question. My mom hung up with a well-rehearsed "I'll have to call you back."

Dad told her that he found the Babies along with Patricia and Aidan Lennon lying in the middle of Monroe Street. She glowered at the two and asked them what they thought they were doing. Donna, the blonde cherub and six year old spokesperson explained patiently that they were trying to make the cars crash. Barb and I stood in the kitchen doorway and snickered. *They're going to get it now,* we predicted. Mom yelled, "I am going to clobber you. Sit on those dining room chairs and don't move until I tell you."

My dad seethed. His job was sacrosanct and he had been embarrassed in front of his captain. He was a quiet, private man with an exemplary sense of duty. His word was his vow.

"Goddammit, Helen, why can't you control these kids?"

"Shaaddup—listen, you try taking care of four kids living in this dump. I told you I wanna move."

My dad threw up his hands, exasperated. He admonished the Babies, "Don't move until I get home," and stalked back to the buggy, shaking his head.

Barb and I weren't surprised at all. Although they looked innocent enough, we knew those Babies were out of control. We often asked each other, "Why did they have them anyway? Everything was fine before." We had spotted these two as trouble early on. Even as infants in diapers they seemed to be up to something, scheming and plotting some new trick. When she was still crawling, Donna had demonstrated her prowess at driving my mother over the edge by eating glass Christmas ornaments. Jackie countered by getting into the family "junk" drawer and consuming staples, pins, and rosary beads. Because the two kids had a limited vocabulary and could only say "Pin", our pediatrician advised daily x-rays until the metal hors d'oeuvres passed the colon. It cost my parents plenty.

Another day, Mom realized the pair went missing. In a panic, she had us searching the apartment and, eventually, our block. Finally, we heard faint giggling in the pantry and found the Babies sitting on the top shelf, eating peanut butter from a jar. No wonder Mom was stressed. She never pretended to like domestic chores, and made no secret of the fact that she hated cooking. We pondered why more kids—especially after a hiatus of five years? Things seemed to have been going smoothly. Later my mom would sometimes explain the second group of progeny as an attempt to have a boy. My dad had one sister, his father was dead and playboy Uncle George, the only other male, had never married and had no children. Who would carry on the Solick family name? But that didn't make sense to Barb and me. Dad said that he liked having daughters. We never got a straight answer, but it seemed like Mom started to unravel when these two Babies came along.

Mom sometimes talked about going back to work. With two more mouths to feed there were fights about money and moving. Living in the apartment was free since Dad was a part owner and he did not want to take on a mortgage or the upkeep of a house. Mom would often reminisce about her college days during the War years and working as a cub reporter for the "Trib." She loved to write and had a talent for it. But she gave up her career aspirations when my dad returned from serving in the South Pacific, and, like many women of that era, she got married and had children. My parents and all their friends got married the same year and started families. I thought maybe they were trying to replace the friends and family they lost in World War II and fill the empty space with children. Mom would talk about how the war had impacted the neighborhood and how so many homes had a star in the window for a loved one who had died in battle in some faraway place. She talked about a boyfriend who drowned in a rice patty when his jeep overturned.

Mom liked to remember the good days and continued to fantasize about what might have been a glamorous career for her entire life. She faithfully watched competitive ice skating and the Olympics because she had dreamed of being another Sonja Henie when she was a girl. She loved musicals and dancing. Later, when I was grown and had moved west, we would see a show together whenever I was in town. When she was in her seventies, we saw a pre-Broadway run of *Chicago*. During one of the numbers, she leaned over to me and said, "See, that's what I always wanted to do." "What?" I whispered. "Be a chorus girl on Broadway." "But these darn varicose veins!" She did not see the incongruity—she was 5' 3" and past retirement. She still thought she could compete with the surgically altered showgirls on stage. She always thought of herself as seventeen.

So maybe diapering babies and chasing kids was never Mom's forte. And those babies definitely gave her a run for her money. She hated staying alone in the apartment nights that Dad was on duty at the firehouse. Mom would let us stay up pretty late, but eventually would shoo us off to bed when she tired of our company. We all went to bed except Jackie. He wasn't ready. Then just a toddler, he got up and found a pair of my dad's wing tips in the hall closet. He donned the shoes and snuck into the living room where Mom dozed on the couch. Jackie hid behind the heavy green palm frond printed draperies and waited for the proper moment. Before he could spring out, Mom woke up, saw a pair of man's shoes peeping from the curtain hem and started screaming! Barb and I, who slept in the master bedroom of our railroad car apartment, ran to her defense, also shrieking at the top of our lungs. Jackie pulled the drapes and emerged, entering center stage, chuckling. Characteristically indulgent, Mom thought this night fright was very funny and told all her friends about his prank.

Barb and I marveled at how our mom could talk—to anyone, about anything. We would get bored, rolling our eyes, waiting for her to finish her gab fest with the albino newspaper man on the corner or some other neighborhood character. Inevitably, we looked for some entertainment during her marathon talk sessions. At age two, I disappeared from my stroller when Mom got into a conversation with some crony in Neisner's dime store. When she realized I was missing, she had store clerks, customers, and the manager searching the premises. They all thought I got out of the store and was hit by a car on Madison Street or kidnapped. The search party finally found me sitting behind the candy counter in a bin of jelly beans, gorging myself on sweets.

It was like déjà vu when the Babies escaped from Mom's gaze at Goldblatt's Department Store. Goldblatt's was one of the first discount stores in Chicago and sold everything from apparel to appliances. They even had a pet department. The store was not as nice as upscale Madigan's, but there was more variety. Mom loaded the Babies in the pram and walked to Crawford and Madison. Barb and I skipped along beside her, window shopping and nagging Mom for candy. When we got to Goldblatt's, she headed for the second floor, where she bumped into an old friend from high school. Barb and I figured this would be a long wait so we asked if we could go to the toy department. "Sure, yeah," she brushed us off —Mom hated to be interrupted when she was talking. Off we went.

Sometime in the middle of her soliloquy, the Babies got fed up, too. Donna went first, over the edge of the buggy, slipping to the linoleum floor. Then she helped with Jackie's escape. Mom didn't notice the Babies were gone, but the guinea pig running along the aisle caught her attention. She laughed and poked fun at the department store management for their laxity. Then she noticed a Capuchin monkey, wearing rayon women's panties on his head, parading towards the escalator. Soon he was followed by a menagerie of pets—parakeets, rabbits, cats, dogs, mice, hamsters, chameleons, snakes, and more monkeys bringing up the rear. All at once it dawned on her; the Babies were the liberation army. Always animal lovers, they had opened every cage in the store and let the animals loose to roam free. Mom collared the tots by the fish tanks and deposited them back in the carriage. She beat it out of Goldblatt's, stopping only to collect Barb and me from the toy department. We never knew how Goldblatt's employees caught all the runaways.

Maybe she was just tired of taking care of four kids, maybe it was disillusionment; a case of the blues as she watched her dreams and her neighborhood fade. We really didn't know why, but it seemed to Barb and me that discipline was getting lax around the house. Although we found them amusing and treated them like our little mascots, we knew the Babies could get away with a lot more than we could. They reminded us of the wisecracking midgets in the *Little Rascals* films. They looked cute, but they had a genius for mischief. They loved to go for the shock value.

Donna and Jackie were the ringleaders of a gang of younger kids. Tito the Gypsy, Aidan and Patricia Lennon and the Babies were always up to some stunt. Once Jackie jumped off the Lennon's second story balcony, trying to fly like Superman. He landed on his head on the concrete, miraculously unscathed except for a small puncture wound. But he bled profusely. Barb and I were curled up on the sofa watching *Saturday Night at the Movies* when a blood soaked Jackie staggered into the living room. We screamed in horror and rushed to his aid. He smirked and then began laughing at us until he choked. He told us he had waited to come home until the blood covered his head and shirt because he wanted to scare us.

There were regular reports of the Babies' capers. There was the time when an overweight woman appeared at our front door, complaining that my brother and sister had slapped her on her ample buttocks, singing, "Babaloo, bongo drums, Ricky Ricardo." Or the time when a mother called to complain that the Babies had tried to convince her kids that a turd of unknown origin was a Tootsie roll on a stick. They had tried to get her children to eat the mystery item, but the smell put them off. Barb and I agreed that we would have been punished, but all the Babies got was a short stint on the dining room chairs, until the phone rang.

Donna and Jackie had the upper hand. When Mom had me babysit for short periods while she ran to the store, they would immediately set out to trash the apartment. If I threatened them and told them to clean up they taunted me with, "We don't have to. We won't get in trouble, she left YOU in charge. You do it." I knew they had me. These kids had no respect. When my parents and my aunt got into a dispute over an oriental rug that escalated into a legal dispute over the restaurant dividends, Donna and Jackie decided they would get revenge. Every time Aunt Marie left her apartment, a shower of rocks and pennies rained from our third story back porch. Donna and Jackie made it their mission to pelt her because "she was mean."

One of their most outrageous escapades was when they decided to become eviction enforcers. Mrs. Lennon had rented her basement to an Irish bachelor named Heavey. The dank basement was hardly a fit living space with its one damp room, a sink, toilet and stall shower, but the tenant wasn't picky and just wanted a place to sleep off his stupors. However, Heavey drank up the modest rent most months and Mrs. Lennon, usually a patient soul, grew tired of feeding the drunken single man. She complained to the kids, "I wish I could just get that paddy out of there." Donna and Jackie decided they could be of service.

Assembling the gang, they hatched a plot to get rid of Heavey forever. They waited until the Irishman left for his breakfast pint at the Shamrock Tavern. Then they ordered Patricia to get the keys to the apartment from the hook in the kitchen and to bring anything slippery that they could find. The four kids let themselves in and proceeded to systematically wreck the place. They emptied the contents of the old ice box on the floor. They poured a sack of flour on the sofa; they pulled the covers off the bed, tore up newspapers, spilled pop on the floor, and tore down the curtains. They were pretty sure that Heavey would move on after viewing the wreckage, but just to make sure they poured shampoo in the stall shower so he would "slip and break his neck."

My friend, Mary Lennon, older sister of Patricia and Aidan, broke the news to me. "You have to come over and see what those brats did. They destroyed Heavey's apartment." I knew immediately which brats she was talking about—it could only be the Babies and their pals. But I was not prepared for the mess I saw when Mary and I opened the door. It looked like a hurricane hit it. It resembled the wreck of the Hesperus. We looked around, looked at each other and said. "Let's get outta here before they make us clean it up. Jinx, you're it."

Barb and I never learned if the basement was cleaned up or if Heavey went on living in the squalid mess. We knew that the Babies never got in any trouble for this act of mayhem. The next thing we heard they'd been chased out of the Marbro Theater for dancing on the stage.

Years later, when she was complaining about some neighbor kid, I asked my mother why she and my dad had children. "You really didn't seem to like them."

"No, you're right," she responded. "Your father and I talked about that and we decided we could have been happy, just the two of us, working and traveling, and going out on the town. But it was what people did then. We were young and full of hope." I wasn't at all surprised. It's what people have done and will do when reclaiming their lives from the devastation of war.

Aidan's Road Trip

Aidan was on a mission.

The two year old scion of the shanty Irish family, the Lennons, headed out in his little red fire truck. Pedaling furiously, clad in his standard issue loaded diaper, the waif made tracks down the brick alley behind his house. He was headed for parts unknown. I didn't know what time he started out. My dad often saw Aidan heading down Madison Street when he left for the firehouse in the wee hours. Rain or shine, winter or summer, if Aidan wasn't playing in the alley, he was barreling around in the fire truck. As it would turn out, this day was different and Aidan was up for a new adventure.

I marveled that a child could be so dirty and still be alive. The thirty-six inch tall tyke was always scantily dressed and looked like he had never seen the inside of a bathtub. He was a towhead, but it was hard to tell under all that muck what his hair color was. He was fair-skinned like most Irish children, but the grime made him look like he had been hanging out on a tropical beach. His head seemed too large for his body. My sister and I called him "Potato Ears." He didn't care.

I thought Aidan was born in a soiled diaper. His uniform changed from summer to winter simply by adding something brown with ear flaps that served as a hat, along with his greasy parka. Aidan liked to play in the cardboard boxes that littered the alley behind our house. I never knew where he might pop up. Once, he almost gave a truck driver a heart attack when the driver drove over a cardboard box that Aidan was playing in. The burly diver, visibly shaken, began to cry because he thought he had crushed the scamp. Miraculously, Aidan was unscathed and crawled away like some grimy Sweetpea. He was made of iron. He was an explorer. He was invincible.

My marvel was not limited to Aidan, however. I marveled at the entire family—the six children and their parents. They confounded me. I could not figure out how they thrived. Mary, the eldest, was a year older than me. I met her in sixth grade after the family moved from Ireland to Liverpool and finally to Chicago by way of Canada. They moved in across the alley from us. When Mary and I became best friends, I got to know the entire family. As was standard practice in those days, Mary was held back because she came from another country even though she was a lot smarter and mature than I was. She had already entered puberty and looked like a middle aged Irish washerwoman at 13.

The Lennon children—Mary, John, Katherine, James, Patricia and Aidan—ranged in age from two to thirteen.

There were plenty of new friends to go around for my two sisters, my brother, and I. The older and younger kids partnered up, but Aidan, being the youngest, was often left behind. The Lennons had lived in other countries, and to us, even if they were grimy; they were sophisticated, exotic and interesting. They told us about life in Ireland, England, and Canada (comma use) and made it sound wonderful—they stoked our dreams of visiting foreign lands. In exchange, we Solick's had clean sheets, costumes, books, and grandparents who would visit with candy and goodies to share. No one was ever turned away from our apartment.

The Lennon house was a ramshackle frame dump, and it suited the family perfectly. It had a tiny kitchen downstairs, a cupboard, a living room, and a bedroom. There were bedrooms upstairs. I never knew how many—I never went up there. I was warned by my mother, under pang of contracting a terrible disease, to "Stay out of that pigsty," after she had visited Mrs. Lennon only one time. The place was so dilapidated and filthy that I didn't need the warning. One look said it all. Mrs. Lennon, a kind, easy going, slovenly lady with a thick brogue who hailed from the auld sod, cautioned us not to play the piano because, "Those little divvils, the mice, will come out." Sometimes I thought she was crazy and other times plain simple. Mrs. Lennon really believed in banshees and the little people and regaled us with fantastic tales from her perch on a chair in the kitchen. The kids ran in and out of the house and when they wanted something they said, "Give us some money," and Mrs. Lennon reached in her pocket and gave them whatever sum they wanted. Money was never an issue but I wasn't sure if they actually had running water.

The house had very little furniture. In the living room there was a broken down sofa with springs hanging out, and besides the piano that served as a home to the mice—no other furniture. There was no dining room, and no one ever sat down to eat. The two younger kids slept in the downstairs bedroom with their parents, and the four older siblings slept upstairs. The beds were never made, and it looked like the sheets were never washed. The kids said there were bats upstairs. Mary said one got in her long hair. The same pot of potatoes that sat in gray water was always boiling on the stove. This might have been the reason for the singular stench that pervaded the house. Mrs.

Lennon generously offered to poke a spud out of the pot for us each time we visited. "No, thank you, Mrs. Lennon," we always replied.

Underwear the color of peat, and fading laundry hung on the line for months until the Lennons discarded the clothes and bought more. The backyard was a cement pad where we played games and practiced our acts for the annual school talent show. We hooked up a record player with an extension cord for our musical accompaniment.

Mr. Lennon owned a bar where the "turkeys," as my Gramps called the Irish men who were fresh off the boat, hung out. The house also had what passed for a basement apartment. There was one squalid room with a shower that served as a living room, kitchen and bedroom. It was there that the drunken Irish bachelors who worked in Mr. Lennon's bar slept off their benders. Mrs. Lennon was always trying to get rid of them. When an arsonist set the basement on fire my Dad, a fireman, asked my mother, "Does Mrs. Lennon take in laundry?" He had never seen so many soiled clothes in his life. The Lennons would wear the clothes until they were stiff, and then pitched them in the basement. Although Mrs. Lennon had a washing machine, it had never seen active duty. She claimed it ruined the clothes and that hand wash (which never actually occurred) was better.

It was anything goes across the alley. There were no rules. Everyone knew it. Old Rosie, the neighborhood recluse, would walk into the Lennons and help herself to anything she wanted: food, clothing, anything. When I witnessed this and expressed my amazement, Mrs. Lennon responded that Rosie was a "pore old soul" and was to be pitied. I thought Rosie had a good thing going. It was in this that Aidan flourished.

One day Aidan fell off the second story landing onto the cement. He had a bump the size of an ostrich egg on his head. My mother was horrified and urged Mrs. Lennon to take him to the doctor. "Oh no, it's just a wee little bump," she replied, "I'll put some butter on it." She slapped a pat of butter on the egg. Aidan rode off in his fire truck, salty butter dripping down his forehead. My sister Barbara and I called him, "Potato Ears" but now we took to calling him, "Egghead." He was a regular breakfast plate and he was shatterproof.

Maybe Aidan took to the road to escape the chaos at home. Or it could have been that the older kids paired up and palled around together and Aidan, by virtue of his tender age, was left alone. The merchants on Madison Street chuckled at the tot and often gave him handouts of candy or day old donuts. Maybe he took off in search of treats. Or perhaps something fueled his dreams of foreign lands. The day Aidan took his long ride, the weather was unusually mild and he started out early. I later speculated about the route he took, but he didn't tell. He was only two and didn't talk much. I thought that he pedaled down the alley past the restaurant loading dock, past the back of the Con Ed office, past the laundromat, and past the Hot Diggity Dog garbage cans.

When he reached Keeler Avenue, I guessed that, instead of making his customary left turn, he proceeded across Keeler, and continued down the alley to Karlov Avenue, near the Off the Street Club where I hung out after school. Past garbage cans and back yards, packing boxes, and finally through trash and fire escapes, Aidan pressed on. A sewer rat scampered by, but Aidan took no notice. Then he made a left turn and headed north to Madison Street. He crossed Karlov and turned right at the Woolworth's rather than crossing at the Neisner's Dime Store. At Neisner's, they sold cardboard pizza and pickles out of a barrel that the kids spat in. Onward he pushed heading east on Madison Street. He passed store after store, lampposts and parking meters, newsstands and record stores. When he got to Crawford, he finally had to stop for the traffic light. He was on a roll.

He crossed the four lanes of traffic to the north side of Madison and continued past the Walgreen's Drug Store, parking lots, and Goldblatt's Department Store, Mayblossom McDonald's Dance Studio, and the notorious Alex Theater. Finally, he reached Garfield Park—the end of his journey.

Garfield Park—it spanned 185 acres and had once been the centerpiece of the Chicago City Parks system. It was completed in 1934 but the conservatory dated from 1908 and was avant-garde in its time. My family considered it the east border of our neighborhood. When my sister and I were toddlers, my mother, a tireless walker, would take long strolls with the baby carriage. After we walked for miles, she would stop for a cigarette. I loved passing time in formal gardens, especially the lily ponds. I often imagined being a fairy and sunning myself on a leaf. Barbara, who was a precocious artist, sketched the water lilies and flowers. It was idyllic. As time passed, we could no longer visit Garfield Park because it became dangerous. There were often reports of muggings, and our mother cautioned we might get "jumped."

That day, Aidan rolled along past the lush kaleidoscope —the conservatory, the lagoons, the pavilion, the botanical and formal gardens, the lily ponds and trickling waterways, the field houses, the tennis courts, the basketball courts, and the gold domed administration building. It was early afternoon before anyone missed him. Since he wandered the neighborhood at will most days, no one took notice when he was gone longer than usual.

Mary came to the back door of our apartment, red faced, with tears in her eyes, "Aidan's gone. He's been kidnapped." I knew that couldn't be true. *No one would touch that kid. They'd have to give him a bath or wear gloves before they would pick him up,* I thought. Even though I was skeptical that anyone would take the urchin, I pretended (tried?) to sympathize and agreed to join in the search. I began scouring the neighborhood, calling his name, checking out every cardboard box and behind every trash can— his usual haunts. I dug around in the discarded floral displays behind Gibbons–O'Keefe Funeral Parlour. Nothing—there was no sight of Aidan as it approached dark.

I never really knew how he made it to Garfield Park, miles and miles away from his house, or how he escaped drowning in the lagoon, avoided being eaten by carp or was not hit by a car. Hours passed. Then, the phone rang at about 8:00 pm in the Lennon home. It was the Garfield Park Police Station. They had apprehended Aidan. He was seen riding his fire truck around the park and a Good Samaritan notified the cops. They brought the little vagabond to the station and ended his latest escapade. Mary came to our apartment door and told us the good news—their darling little Aidan had been found.

The next day I opened the neighborhood newspaper to the front page and laughed so hard my stomach hurt. I ran to show my mother and sister and they screamed, shaking with amazement. There, on the front page, was a picture of errant Aidan, beaming from the top of the front desk at the Garfield Park Police Station. Chicago cops surrounded him. He held the remains of a melting chocolate ice cream cone in his hand; most of it had found his face and chest. He was indestructible.

Tito and the Gypsies

The hand lettered particle board sign read:

FORTUNE TELLING TEA LEAVES READ
COUNSELING ON YOUR ROMANCE MONEY
CRYSTAL BALL TAROT CARDS PAST LIVES

The black and red letters jumped off the white background. I watched as the gypsies hung the sign by ropes from the second story window over the coffee shop at Madison and Keeler. The sign looked exotic and mysterious to my childish eyes. I envisioned a darkened studio - beaded curtain, crystal balls, heavy draperies, and a beautiful woman in a turban and brocade skirts. I could almost smell the incense. It smelled like the incense that the priest used in church.

Mom didn't think the sign was exotic or mysterious, just another confirmation that the neighborhood was on the skids. I pleaded with her to let me visit the fortune teller, knowing this wouldn't happen.

"Mom, Mom, pulleeeeze? Can't I go to the fortune teller? I want to find out what my math grade will be. It's only a dollar"

"You know what your math grade will be—B-. No, absolutely not, stay away from those gypsies. They are thieves and con artists."

"But they can tell the future."

"No they can't. They are clever at getting people to tell them things about themselves."

"Well, what about Maleva? She saw the future."

"Who?

"You know the gypsy in *The Wolf Man*. She saw that pentagram on Lon Chaney's hand."

"Oh, you mean Maria Ouspenskaya? She is Russian and it's an act. Don't let me catch you hanging around that fortune telling parlor."

"But Carole Dowling's Mom said she could go."

My friend Carole Dowling's parents were declared "permissive" by Mom. I knew this argument would not work but thought I would give it a shot anyway.

"Carole Dowling's Mom lets her do anything and go anywhere. That kid is going to get in trouble, you mark my words. Subject closed—the answer is no."

When we arrived for school the next day Sister Frances Anne was raging. She held forth about fortune telling and divination for at least 20 minutes through most of our morning math class. I hoped she'd go on all day.

"It is the work of the devil. Only God is omniscient."

"It is a mortal sin to ask someone to tell you the future."

And the final threat. "You will go to hell."

I rolled my eyes and snickered. The nun couldn't see me sitting in the first row, first seat. Her habit blocked her view. I thought Sister Frances Anne was nuts. I disliked her intensely since she made me take my Kennedy campaign buttons off my uniform before I entered her classroom. I hated her so much that I was happy when I got the flu and couldn't come to school for two weeks. I hoped that she'd go on with her diatribe until the bell ran for us to go home, so I goaded her. She took the bait.

"But if God created gypsies and gave them the gift to see the future, then shouldn't we have our fortunes told, Sister Frances Anne?"

"Haven't you heard a thing I said, young lady, fortune telling is blasphemy and the devil's work. Gypsies are the devil's handmaidens."

I winked and nodded to my friends just out of Sister's range of vision as she ranted about eternal damnation.

"This should be good for at least a couple of hours—maybe even into the geography lesson."

The threats about consorting with gypsies had no effect on the Babies, Donna and Jack. They did not discriminate. They immediately befriended Tito, the five-year-old son of the fortune tellers. He was a short kid, olive skin, and curly hair. Donna and Jack met him in the dirt lot behind the apartment building on Monroe Street where the Goldufskys lived. All the kids played in the lot— baseball, tag, hide-and-go-seek. In bygone years, the lot sported a lawn, but the slum landlord abandoned watering the grass a long time ago. It was the perfect spot for kids to meet and hang out. Tito introduced himself to the pair.

"Hi, do you want to play?"

That was all the Babies needed to add Tito to their gang. They palled around with Katherine, Aidan, and Patricia Lennon, Tito, and Medina. Although Medina was Mexican, and his parents spoke no English, the Babies insisted Samuel Medina's name was McDina and he was Irish. Mom again warned them to stay away from the gypsies, but her admonitions fell on deaf ears.

"He is a nice kid, we like him," the Babies always replied.

That was that. He was part of the gang. Eventually, Mom relented and Tito was invited into our apartment. Mom liked to hold forth on any subject and even Tito did not escape being an audience for her musings.

Yet another blow for urban decay was struck, when the Community Discount Store opened down the block on Madison Street. My parents were livid.

"It's a junk shop," Mom declared

Dad corroborated, "They get their stock from army surplus and fire sales." As a Chicago fireman, we knew he had the straight scoop

We kids were not deterred by their review. The store advertised a grand opening with hot dogs and balloons. We all traipsed down the street, arm in arm, quarters in hand, to check out the bargains. The older kids, I, Barb, Mary Lennon, and Donna Doyle led the parade. The little kids followed us, Donna, Jack, Katherine, Tito, Patricia, Aidan, and McDina. We made sure they held our hands crossing Madison Street. We entered the front door of the storefront.

I knew in an instant my parents were right. It was a junk shop. Everything smelled like smoke and had telltale water marks. Odds and ends lined the shelves. Old gas masks, canteens, and army fatigues shared space with ladies' girdles, past dated canned food, and mismatched hose. Then we spied the bargain of the day: HULA HOOPS – 10 cents, 12 for a buck.

The hula hoop craze came and went about two years before the big opening of Community Discount. When we bought our hula hoops originally, they cost two dollars apiece. Now they were passé, but the hula hoops were the best deal. Tito told us he had never had one. Any money he made was turned over to his parents. The gang bought out their stock of the fluorescent fad toys, small and large, and hauled out booty home.

After a few twirls in the Lennon's' backyard, I was bored.

"Here Tito, it's yours."

Tito beamed. "Thanks!"

He ran back home to the fortune telling parlor with his bounty. I saw him every day, skipping down Madison Street with the hula hoop. Maybe it was his only toy.

Everyone in Tito's family pulled in money and the five-year-old was no exception. A real entrepreneur, he would get a stock of plastic flowers, we never know from where, and set up shop on the corner of Madison and Keeler on Sundays when families frequently visited the cemeteries and graves of loved ones.

Dad rented a garage from the Bauers who lived on Monroe Street. He parked his prized 1957 pink and silver Chevy Bel Air in the garage. The car was his pride and joy. He washed and waxed the car by hand and would not let anyone touch it. When the family went for a Sunday outing, Dad would pull the car into the alley from the rented garage, head west to Kildare, turn right on Kildare, then right again on Madison. We'd watch for him to pull up in front of the restaurant. We'd run the three flights of stairs. Dad did not like to be kept waiting, but Mom was always late, and he was already fuming when we loaded up in the car to head out to the country and Cedar Lake.

Weekly, as Dad pulled up to the stop light to make our right turn on Keeler, Tito jumped out of nowhere with a bunch of plastic flowers in his hand. He grabbed hold of the handle on the driver's side door and hung on for dear life. Dad slammed on the brakes and exploded. His eyes looked like they would pop out of his head.

"Get that goddamn kid off my car. Son of a bitch, he's gonna get killed."

Dad rolled down the window.

"Buy some flowers, Mister?"

"Get off my car."

"Mister, buy some flowers."

"Get off. Go home. Get back on the sidewalk."

Finally, Tito relented and backed off, returning to the abandoned newsstand where he kept his stock of plastic flowers. Dad kept swearing most of the way to Cedar Lake.

"Why is that kid in the street? He's gonna get run over. Goddamn gypsy brat. I should call the Child Welfare office. Helen, why don't you do something?"

"Me? You call 'em."

Donna and Jack continued to chant until Dad finally simmered down.

"He's a nice kid. He's a nice kid. We like him."

Hot Diggity Dog

"Hot diggity, dog diggity, boom/ What you do to me."

The gang sang the popular ditty as we cruised down the cobblestone alley, our little Appian Way between Madison and Monroe Streets. The alley was our playground—it backed all our houses and was our thoroughfare to adventure.

There were thirteen of us: The Lennons—Mary, John, Katherine, Patricia, and Aidan, the Solicks—me, Barb, Donna, and Jack, Samuel McDina, Donna Doyle, her younger brother David Doyle, and Tito the Gypsy. We were headed to the grand opening of the new Chicago style hot dog stand on Keeler Avenue next to the laundromat. Capitalizing on the popularity of the song, the proprietors had named the grimy take out place, "Hot Diggity Dog."

The gang was eager to check out this new food venue. Marginal small businesses—fortune tellers, junk shops, Chinese takeout with a gambling parlor in the backroom—occupied vacated store fronts as more established businesses took flight from our neighborhood for greener pastures. Before the Hot Diggity Dog opening, the owners tried to generate enthusiasm and showered the neighborhood with leaflets. The hand-painted stencil window sign promised free soft serve ice cream, dogs, balloons, and door prizes. Excited, we alternated between a running and skipping down the alley, anticipating our free treats. Disregarding our mother's standard warning, "The place has rats. You'll get ptomaine," we were ready with our coupons in hand for free eats.

In July, when every day seemed like the last day of Pompeii, a free cone sounded like a great idea. But as we turned the corner our maniacally eager expressions vanished. The line to get free soft serve cones stretched all the way around the corner on Madison Street right up to the front door of Solick's restaurant. It looked like every kid in the neighborhood had heard about the freebies. I wanted to throw in the towel and go to Columbus Park swimming pool. I didn't like vanilla cones anyway. I wanted a chocolate dip cone. If we hurried, I argued, we'd still make the last batch of 500 kids before they closed the pool for cleaning. But the rest of the gang maintained that free ice cream was worth the delay.

"Come on, Anita, the line isn't that long. It's moving fast."

I really didn't want to go to the pool alone so I reluctantly agreed to hang out and wait my turn in the heat and humidity of Chicago in July.

As we walked past the takeout joint to claim our places in line, I had time to size up the place. I had to agree with my mother. Hot Diggity Dog didn't look too hot. I admired their entrepreneurship, though. The staff was sweating and working as fast as they could, taking orders and dishing out soft serve to overheated customers. Their aprons were stained and the trash cans were overflowing. Money and sawdust covered the linoleum. The owners had developed their own creative security system. They figured it would be harder to rip the place off if thieves had to pick up the cash and instructed the customers to throw their money on the floor.

Sweaty dogs spun on the greasy roller rotisserie—no sneeze guard in sight. Mom was probably right about the hygiene. I saw people walking past us with cones and Chicago dogs and remembered my mother's cautionary tales about dirty kitchens and diseases you'd get if you weren't careful. The pungent smell of the dogs and the raw onions and the bleach smell from the laundromat next door made me gag. I thought about all the nasty pig body parts that were supposed to be in hot dogs. Maybe those hot peppers really were cockroaches—were they wiggling? I needed a Coke.

Feeling queasy, I decided to pass on the cone and gave my coupon to Tito the Gypsy. It just wasn't worth the risk of getting sick when I wasn't in school. I waited in line for my buddies to get their free cones. To pass the time I practiced my tap dance and Ethel Merman imitation, belting out, "I got rhythm..." until my friends began hitting me to make me stop. I felt like my brain was boiling. I started to perspire and black lines formed in the creases of my knees and elbows. We got to the front door—the dogs were sizzling and so were we. Finally, we reached the counter and everyone got their cones. We ran all the way to Columbus Park in time to join 487 other kids for the last splash at the pool that day.

The next day, the gang hooked up in search of new adventures. It was the middle of summer and we were beginning to get bored. The first day of school was still over a month away. I pinched myself. Could I really be wishing I were back in school? Was it heat stroke? I decided I better rest and get myself a lime Popsicle. As the gang strolled down the alley between Madison and Monroe musing about what we could do for fun that day, I spied an amazing treasure—perched on top of the garbage can was a whole box of the coupons for free ice cream! The gang went wild! What a score!

"Best day ever!"

There were at least 500 coupons in the box. It would keep us all in free ice cream all summer. I had another idea. I tried reasoning with the gang.

"We could sell the coupons and make some money."

They voted me down.

"You're crazy. It says free. Who'd pay for it?"

"We could sell them for a penny a pop—that's five bucks!"

"Nawww. Ice cream. Ice cream," they chanted.

I steadfastly maintained that we could sell them at a significant discount to kids and contended that since I saw them first I had first right of disposal. I couldn't persuade the gang that the coupons were solely mine and this would be a better idea than eating 500 ice cream cones.

"We all saw them at the same time. They belong to all of us."

To keep the peace, I decided that I would just go with this communist spirit. But then I saw a potential problem and pointed it out to the gang.

"The coupons say '1 to a customer.' And we went yesterday."

"We'll disguise ourselves. They will never recognize us!"

"With what? It's not Halloween."

"We can trade clothes and stuff."

I doubted that the staff would be fooled by this juvenile masquerade, but agreed to help out. I had nothing better to do. We decided to test the waters and see if we could fool the Hot Diggity Dog staff. So we marched in and presented our coupons. We were surprised when the man behind the counter did not balk. Everyone got their cones—I gave mine to Mitzy, the Lennon's mongrel dog. The cones were either consumed or melted in minutes. We decided to try again. I put on sunglasses and my sister and I switched scarves and tied them around our hair which we pulled into pony tails. Tito turned his shirt backwards. The entire gang tried to disguise their appearance. I surveyed the young grifters. The results looked pretty dismal. Always the skeptic, I doubted our chances of success.

"It'll never work."

The gang agreed we should give it a shot. Boldly we marched up to the counter of Hot Diggity Dog. I shushed the younger kids who were giggling. I presented the first coupon and, without a blink, the man behind the counter handed me a cone. The gang filed up, winking and nodding. I wondered whether he just didn't care because working at Hot Diggity Dog was such a lousy job or if he really had lost his marbles because of the heat and did not recognize us. We all marched out choking back the laughter. Back in the alley, we jumped in the air and yelled and congratulated each other. Mitzy got another cone, and licked the cobblestones in the alley after she'd polished it off.

This charade went on day after day. I was an early defector. I didn't like vanilla and pretty soon got bored with the game. Eventually the older kids gave up, tired of the same old vanilla cones. The thrill was gone. Fickle fans that we were we decided a pizza slice at the dime store was our new favorite. The soda fountain at the drugstore advertised fresh limeade. A Greek takeout opened in the next block later that summer and they served the greasiest fries I'd ever seen. Cooked in olive oil, almost transparent and served in wax paper; they were a salty taste treat.

One by one, the kids switched their allegiances. We forgot about the free cones. But Aidan, the little waif, soldiered on. Breakfast, lunch, and dinner, I'd watch him from my third story wooden back porch. He pedaled down the alley in his fire truck to Hot Diggity Dog, coupon in hand. I'd yell to him.

"Aidan! Getting a cone?"

He'd waive and nod.

Aidan pedaled right through the front door of Hot Diggity Dog, clutching his greasy meal ticket. Not a word was exchanged between him and the man behind the counter. The short order cook turned to the soft serve machine and had the cone ready by the time Aidan reached the stools. They had an understanding.

I watched him pedal back, winter and summer, ice cream dripping down his dirty t-shirt onto his perpetually grimy diaper. A fatter Mitzy trotted next to him, catching the drips. Aidan grinned from ear to dirty ear.

Saturday at the Movies

Every Wednesday night I had a routine. Before I went to bed I climbed over the arm of the brown overstuffed easy chair in the corner and lifted the sash window. Although the concrete pavement loomed three stories below, I bravely hung my head out, craned my neck, and leaned sideways to check the Marbro marquee, ablaze in white lights. The usher still in his braided uniform, teetered on his ladder, cigarette pinched in the corner of his mouth, while he replaced one letter after another.

My younger sister, Barb, anxiously tugged at my pajama leg, "What does it say, what does it say?"

Mom, interrupted her telephone call for a moment, warning, "You'll crack your skull again!" and then called out, "What's playing?"

Impatient for the mystery to be revealed, I tapped my feet, and tried to guess the new feature, as the usher hung one letter after another on the marquee...H...E...R...could it be Hercules, I wondered?

I whooped and shouted to my younger sister, Barb. "Barb, *Hercules Unchained*! We're going on Saturday."

In the 1950s, television was the new fad. Like all our friends, Barb, and I followed the TV shows of the day—*Ding Dong School*,

Howdy Doody, Mickey Mouse Club, Davy Crockett, Mighty Mouse, and *Superman.* We enjoyed the shows. We'd even appeared on a local kids show, but our real passion was for the movie theaters, big screens, Cinemascope and Todd-AO. The theaters offered us glamour and escape. The fledgling technology consisting of a tiny box with a black and white screen and embryonic production values couldn't rival the Marbro Theater. Even with Winky Dink, TV never held our interest like a movie could.

We kids couldn't see that the era of the movie palaces was over. Beset by competition from free television, falling attendance, and government lawsuits, the theaters were in decline. Blinded by the opulence of bygone days, Barb and I didn't notice the frayed upholstery, dusty drapes, or the worn carpeting. We didn't see that the mirrors needed resilvering or the gilt needed repainting. We thought the theaters really were palaces!

Our toughest decision on a Saturday was which theater to go to. The Marbro, the Paradise, the State Lake, the Byrd, and the Crawford theaters were all within walking distance of our family's apartment. Only one theater was off limits—the notorious Alex Theater.

Movie going was a tradition in our family. Mom and Daddy went to the movies several nights a week. My mother liked to reminisce about their courtship days, and even after a couple of kids arrived, movie going was still a date for my parents. Mom and Daddy were at the Marbro watching *Sunset Boulevard* when Mom went into labor with Barb. But she wouldn't leave until Norma Desmond declared, "I'm ready for my close up, Mr. DeMille," and Mom barely made it to the delivery room on time.

For the big blockbusters like the *Ten Commandments* and *Ben Hur,* our parents would treat us to the lavish downtown movie houses. They'd stand in cold and the long lines, waiting to buy tickets for the first run films, although they could have waited until the movie ran at the Marbro. They were dedicated movie fans, too.

For most of our movie viewing, we attended the same theaters our parents did when they were kids. Mom made us envious when she would reminisce about how the movies cost a nickel when she was a kid. We complained that paying a quarter was unfair—an early lesson in inflation.

Movies were an important part of our lives. Mom filled the lonely nights when Daddy was at the firehouse by taking us to a movie with other firemen's wives and kids. And, Barb and I usually spent our Saturdays in some movie theater or another. With the coming attractions, newsreels, cartoons, and the intermission between the double feature, movie going was an all-day affair.

Movies were my primary source of information and culture. The commercial for the concession stand that ran during intermission was my first exposure to opera and classical music. Cartoons like Brunhilde, the Valkyries, and Toreadors exhorted us to buy more popcorn, candy, sodas, and hot dogs.

Our Saturday routine was always the same. We got up, ate a hearty breakfast of Kellogg's Frosted Flakes, and watched cartoons. Eventually my mother, who was always a night owl and a late riser, got up. Then Gramps appeared on his weekly visit bearing gifts. My grandfather spoiled us with presents and attention. My mother would inevitably gripe that his largesse was to make up for what he had not given her growing up.

Tall, still handsome and always impeccably dressed in a suit, tie, hat and overcoat if the weather was cold, his arms were filled with bags of bakery goods, coffee cakes, six packs of candy, ice cream and toppings from Walgreen's. After Gramps spread out all the goodies on the kitchen table, he slyly dug in his pockets and pulled out dollar bills for the kids. His face betrayed no emotion—he loved to watch the looks on our avaricious little faces as he surreptitiously slid the bills into our greedy little hands as if it were our secret. We whooped with joy. One dollar was a lot of money in those days— more than enough for us to go to the movies. Admission for kids was only a quarter and we already had candy (thanks to Gramps).

Barb and I hurried to dress while we conferred on our movie choices and checked the ratings in the Catholic newspaper, *The New World*. The movies were rated from A– Acceptable for All Audiences, B– Morally Objectionable, and C– Condemned. Disney usually got an A, Marilyn Monroe a B, and Tennessee Williams a C for a mortal sin. If the movie was something we really wanted to see, we would try to hide the newspaper. When my mother asked, we would either reply that "we could not find the paper" or that the movie was so new, "it wasn't listed." That strategy worked for only the films about which she knew nothing. We got three daily newspapers, so it was pretty likely mom knew what the films were about. She nixed films like *Psycho*, *Cat on a Hot Tin Roof*, and pretty much anything that sounded like sex or "adult themes." Violence was okay, and we were allowed to see any western or any horror movie with impunity.

Barb and I would agree on a double or triple feature and head out. There was a Karmelkorn shoppe on the south side of Madison Street, across from the Marbro. I liked regular butter popcorn and Barb liked caramel corn, so each of us bought a box for $0.15 and brought it to the theater. It was way before the days of government regs about bringing food into the theaters. Even after we bought popcorn and our tickets, we still had $0.60 each to get us through the week. We were too young to realize that our thrifty ways would contribute to the demise of our beautiful theaters—we were just stretching our allowance.

The Marbro was one half-city block away and showed films that had already played the downtown theaters. The State Lake usually ran the same bill as the Marbro. The Crawford had triple feature horror films on Saturdays. The Byrd mostly showed films that were in rerelease like *The Jolson Story* or *The Wizard of Oz*. We even went to the legendary Paradise Theater before it was demolished. And what an incredible theater it was.

When it was built the Paradise tried to compete with the Marbro as the flagship theater in our neighborhood. The theater was legendary for its luxurious décor. When Balaban and Katz acquired the Paradise they tried to make it one of the great showplaces in Chicago, adding fantastic ornamentation. The Paradise design featured heavenly bodies and mythological figures throughout. The theater's marquee, one of the largest in Chicago, blazed with a sunburst design and electric lights in ten different colors. The entry was festooned with marble statuary and murals depicting zodiac constellations on the ceiling high above.

I watched the movies at the Paradise surrounded by an imitation night sky, full of twinkling stars, my tiny feet dangling as I sat on the edge of my seat. It was magical—especially when watching movies like *Peter Pan* with Daddy. In the corners of the theater, statues of trumpeting angels heralded the approach of Apollo, the sun god, riding behind a marble chariot with horses over the balcony. If the movie didn't interest me, the décor always did. I'd stare at the constellations on the ceiling and try to pick out Orion, and the Pleiades, and the Big Dipper. The last film that I saw there was *Song of the South* but I never forgot this enchanted place. Sadly, through most of its life, the theater barely broke even and was dismantled in 1956—its beautiful statuary sold to a mafia-run steakhouse.

The Marbro was always the first choice on Saturday afternoons. Seating 4000 people, it was one of the largest movie houses in Chicago and the entertainment anchor of the neighborhood. Even to adult eyes, this was a grand showplace. The exterior was designed in Spanish Baroque style. The theater featured a splendid lobby with a two story staircase like something out of Rhett and Scarlett's home in *Gone with the Wind*. The staircase was lighted by a triple tier crystal chandelier. The balcony had a hall of mirrors that rivaled Versailles. In its glory days, the Marbro had even featured live entertainment.

Although the Solicks were faithful theater patrons and continued their support through the generations, we couldn't hold off the inevitable. Eventually even the glorious Marbro was reduced to competing with TV sets. To give the management credit, they tried every trick to fill the seats. They offered promotional dishware to get patrons in the door, and for a while odd selections of plates and cups graced our cupboard. They booked live acts and guest appearances by "stars".

We flocked to see the Three Stooges live at the Marbro. At the time they were enjoying newfound celebrity because of television revivals of their films from the 1940s. It didn't occur to us kids that they had aged since their heyday. Barb and I were shocked when we ran into them outside the theater. They were older than our parents! Moe had wrinkles and a bald spot on the back of his head. Larry's crop of wiring hair had thinned and the Joe we knew from the films had been replaced by a younger guy. Barb and I laughed and were flattered when they told us to "beat it" when we badgered them for autographs. It seemed it was right in character for those curmudgeonly cutups.

In desperation, the celebrity parade continued. "Live! Spanky! On Stage!" the advertisement read. One week, the Marbro featured a marathon of *Little Rascals* comedies, again, leveraging the popularity of the films because of their television resurrection. Spanky was the featured guest performer. Even though Mom warned us that Spanky was her contemporary, we were unprepared for what happened when we arrived at the theater.

We could not reconcile the image of the wisecracking baby with the man that stood on stage. This hit home hard. As kids in an urban, decaying neighborhood, we identified with the Little Rascals and their antics. Now, we had the supreme disillusionment of seeing that Spanky from *Our Gang* had grown up. He stood on the stage, telling stories from the early days of cinema and we couldn't deny it—he wasn't a cute little kid anymore. He was an overweight adult man on stage who looked more like Spanky's dad. And as he told us stories of what happened to the Little Rascals, we became more and more depressed. He said he was a teacher! We could not believe Alfalfa was dead. Visions of our mortality. What a letdown! We skulked out of the theater that day and Barb and I decided that this time TV had the edge—at least the Mouseketeers were actual kids.

Soon the Marbro resorted to even crazier promotions in an effort to pump up the ticket receipts. We stood with a gang of kids on Madison Street and taunted the muscle man who posed in chains outside the theater when *Hercules Unchained* opened. Barb and I couldn't figure out why he was posing on top of a car and what a Buick had to do with Mount Olympus.

"Are you a mouse or a man?" we screamed at the hapless body builder.

Secretly, we felt a little sorry for him as he braved the Chicago weather clad only in his leopard skin loincloth.

I squealed in delight when theater management pulled out all the stops and the gimmicks to scare us at Castle horror film screening. Skeletons and ghosts were rigged on pulleys and flew through the audience at just right moment during *House on Haunted Hill*. 3D effects added to the thrill. They wired the seats to give electric shocks to the patrons during the screening *of The Tingler*. I was a fan of horror films. Barb was more discerning in her tastes and didn't like the tacky films at all.

She kept her hands over her eyes during most of the movies and I would try to get her to look, entreating, "This is the good part—look, look," My pleas were in vain. Barb was not going to have any nightmares and never opened her eyes. She faithfully sat through the triple feature horror films at the Crawford with me, too. We were sisters and did everything together. While I watched *Creature from the Black Lagoon, It From Beyond Outer Space, I Married a Monster from Outer Space, The Thing,* and *The Blob,* Barb endured patiently with eyes closed until "The End" rolled across the screen.

Our Saturday sojourns to the movies gave Mom a much needed break. We'd be gone almost all day Saturday returning just before dark. With four kids, she needed it. When my younger sister, Donna and younger brother, Jack, known as the Babies, were old enough to accompany us, our mom let us take them to the Marbro. I knew she let us take them anywhere to get them out of her hair for a while. We were cautioned to hold their hands and watch both ways crossing the street. She didn't know that as soon as we crossed the threshold we banished them to the balcony and took off with our friends. We warned them "not to tell or we wouldn't take them again." They were sworn to secrecy and promised to wait for us after the show. In exchange for their freedom, they kept their promise.

But the Babies were a couple of holy terrors and got into mischief if left on their own. Although their sweet and innocent faces did not betray it, they were capable of mayhem. Once, while perched in the balcony, watching a boring remake of *State Fair* with Ann Margaret and Pat Boone, they were inspired to drop water balloons on the patrons below. Since they had no water balloons they decided to improvise. They agreed to make the supreme sacrifice and make do with Carnation chocolate malted milk drinks instead. As we waited for a rare and exciting moment in the film when Ann Margaret protested to Pat about how important her show business career in the carnival was to her, the tots dangled over the balcony railing.

"Ready? One, two, three—go!"

The little darlings pitched the drinks over the side along with a couple of ice cream cones, held their breath, and waited for a reaction. The bombs hit a man with his arm wrapped around his date seated in the orchestra below the balcony. Barb and I, seated below in the orchestra heard the man yell.

"Mother f#$%^r! I am going to kill you assholes!" pealed out across a hushed theater.

The Babies peeped over the balcony to assess the damages. The victim's topcoat and fedora, placed neatly in his lap, were drenched with chocolate goo. His head was plastered with malted milk and Drumsticks, bits of waffle cone stuck to his ears. A platoon of teenage ushers, neighborhood thugs and the older brothers of our friends who liked to bully the younger kids, were employed to keep the peace and eject rowdy patrons. The ushers were dispatched to the balcony to find the troublemakers. Donna and Jack sank even lower into their seats and tried to look younger than 4 and 5.

"Hey you kids, who did that?" demanded the head usher, looking very official in his braided uniform.

"Some big kids did it—they ran that way," the little punks lied straight-faced, suppressing their squeals of delight.

When we collected the brats after the show, they told us the truth and we congratulated them on their prank. Again, we swore them to secrecy, but the story was too funny and we promptly spilled the beans to my mother when we walked in the door. Her eyebrows arched as we told her about the spill and then she let out with a roar of laughter.

"Oh my God, you kids. What did he do? What did he do? Oh my God."

This incident only encouraged Donna and Jack and they began cutting up at the theater on a regular basis. One time, we were amazed to see the pair ride up the center aisle with their pal, Aidan Lennon in his fire truck. The wheels of the truck squeaked as Aidan pedaled up the carpeted ramp to the stage. Donna and Jack jumped on the stage and began singing, "Me and my shadow..." while performing a tap dance.

Adult patrons screamed, "Get off the stage, you brats!" and, again, the ushers led the charge.

But Donna and Jack were too little and too fast. They ran out the side exit and escaped into the alley. Barb and I ran out the main entrance and collected the Babies. They were lying on the sidewalk catching their breath in between laughs while their tiny pal, Aidan, pedaled off in his toy truck.

Movies were my touchstone for history and culture. Thanks to the horror films, I became fascinated with Egypt and mummies. I haunted the Field museum in Chicago on weekends until closing time perusing their Egyptian collection. I bought mini statues of

Bastet and postcards of sarcophagi and fantasized about becoming a paleontologist when I grew up. I watched all the old films on Chicago's Shock Theater. I adored Boris Karloff and was fascinated with the idea that you could achieve everlasting life by drinking a cup of tanna-leaf tea.

In fact, my sympathies were always with the monsters in the movies. They seemed to have so much more class than the smarmy heroes of the films. I couldn't understand why the heroine would choose her wimpy boyfriend over someone who offered eternal life. Even if Boris Karloff was a bit wrinkly, I felt he had a dusty suave dignity that was incredibly engaging. He was a Prince of Egypt after all.

So I was beside myself with joy when I learned that the 1959 film *The Mummy* with Peter Cushing would play in our neighborhood. The Theater advertised that the Mummy himself would appear in person! All my friends were planning to go. What could I do? Of course it was going the play at the Alex—the one theater in our neighborhood was taboo and off limits. It was on the east end of the neighborhood near Garfield Park in a dicey area now considered dangerous. The theater originally known as the Hamlin had begun its life as a vaudeville house. After vaudeville was dead, it was later remodeled to show films. By the 1950s, the theater showed only the cheesiest horror movies. The main reason it was off limits was that it didn't employ ushers and was pure kiddy chaos every weekend. My mother forbade us from going to the Alex.

"No, the place has rats," she responded to our pleas. "The popcorn has cockroaches." "You will get sick—the answer is NO."

I told Mom that it was unfair that my friend, Mary Lennon, could always go to the Alex and nothing happened to her, but Mom wouldn't relent. The Alex was banned. I tried every angle but the answer from her was still no. I badgered her for weeks before the film opened but she wouldn't give in.

I even tried to enlist my grandmother's support to wear my mother down, but Gram, usually my ally, said, "Oh honey, I don't know how you can stand to watch those movies. They frighten me."

I was in a panic. I could not miss this film and a personal appearance by the Mummy.

I had one last chance. When we were kids the telephone that hung on the kitchen wall near the dining room was grafted to my mother's head. When she was talking to her friends, she'd agree to anything not to be interrupted. She'd park on a folding stepstool with her Coke and cigarette and gossip with her old girlfriends from high school and premarriage days. That would be our cue to nag her for concessions. When she was thoroughly engaged in some juicy story, we would start badgering her for something we knew she wouldn't allow if we had her full attention. Barb and I hatched a plot. While Mom was talking with Connie, her best friend for life, I broached the Mummy topic again in a low voice and mumbled something about going to see the film.

"Mom, please, I gotta go..."

"What, what do you want? Yeah, yeah, just go on, okay, just don't bother me, I am on the telephone," she replied.

I had her. She said YES. A few weeks passed and the opening was near. I nervously reminded her that she agreed to let me go.

"I don't remember that," she objected.

"You were on the phone," I replied.

To her credit, she never reneged on those promises we extracted while she was preoccupied with a phone call.

"Oh. Alright. But you are not going to like it. That place is a dump," she warned.

I rejoiced.

For weeks I boned up on my Egyptology by watching the old *Mummy* movies, reading *Classics Illustrated*, and perusing my grade school history book. When the big day finally arrived, Barb and I were excited and nervous. Before we left for the show, Mom took another opportunity to lecture us. She warned about the rats and cockroaches and told us not to go near the restroom because we might be molested by some dirty old man just hanging out trying to grab little girls. The cautionary tale didn't deter us. We were going to see the Mummy in person. We set off east on Madison Street for the Alex, quarters in hand.

Nothing our mother said prepared us for what we saw when we crossed the threshold of the theater. We felt like Orpheus and Eurydice descending into Hades. It was anarchy. The concessions stand looked like it had been ransacked. Fortunately, we had our own treats in our pockets, courtesy of Gramps, because there was no way we would touch anything that came from behind the smudged, greasy glass display cases. The cockroaches didn't have to look far for grub; there was popcorn all over the floor. Sticky soda had dried on the hexagonal tiles of the entry way and our shoes made suctiony noises as we walked into the auditorium. No one took our tickets because Mom was right—there were no ushers.

Barb and I tried to find seats that didn't have the springs hanging out and sat down. We pulled our knees up and sat with our feet on the seat because we didn't want those rats to nibble our toes. And then, the theater doors opened. The kids in the theater began to scream. Slowly, hesitatingly, a guy wrapped in ace bandages and gauze started down the aisle. We screamed too. Then, one kid ran up to him and tried to grab a souvenir, and then another and another.

Like Sebastian in *Suddenly Last Summer*, he was besieged by wild kids. They were trying to rip off the Mummy's bandages!

The Mummy fought back, yelling, "Leave me alone, you goddamn kids!" but they didn't stop.

Finally, he ran out of the auditorium cursing and then the lights went down.

We never heard one word of the film because the kids shrieked at the tops of their lungs throughout the whole movie.

What a bust. We were disgusted. Barb and I agreed we had wasted our quarters. We vowed never go to the Alex again and would only go to the Marbro. Mom was right. Again. We decided to mitigate our disappointment with Green River shakes at the Dutch Mill soda fountain.

That day, we'd had another glorious cinema adventure under our belts, and we thought there would be many more to come. But that was not to be. We could not foresee that the little television boxes would dominate everyone's homes and neglect would doom our beloved Marbro. The theater was demolished in 1963, just four years after the Mummy was stripped and the same year we moved, never to return to Madison Street. Our friends who still lived in the neighborhood described the day they stood across the street and cried when the wrecking ball took the Marbro down.

Hijinks, Heroes and Hellians

Death and Lemonade

Living in our apartment over Solick's Restaurant gave us entrée into a world that was verboten to a lot of the kids we grew up with. We had a crow's nest view of the world and what we lacked in domestic amenities was more than compensated for by our celestial dwelling on the third story of 4207 Madison Street. We had no backyard, just a cement loading dock where the trucks pulled in to deliver groceries and restaurant supplies, and trash was put out for pickup. But we had rooftops and sidewalks and alleys for our playground. We watched an amazing world go by. Weddings, funerals, graduations, robberies, car accidents, New Year's Eve revelers, shoppers, political campaigners, school kids, nuns, street cars, buses—we saw it all. Because my Dad's family owned a restaurant, we had a connection to the business owners in the community—the butcher who had been his Grandfather's competitor, the Greek grocer, the funeral parlor owner, the florist, and the other restaurant and shop owners.

Gibbons–O'Keefe Funeral Parlor was about a half block west of us on Madison Street. The storefront and plain signage did not give a clue to the mysteries that lay within. The reception area paneled in dark wood led to room after room hung with flocked wallpaper, heavy velvet draperies trimmed with fringe and corded ties, needlepoint cushions, and overstuffed couches. Candles and incense smoldered and mixed with traces of musky floral arrangements and embalming fluid. Each family had a separate viewing room and the mortuary also sported a small chapel that served as a gathering place when the priests came to lead prayers for the deceased. The caskets were the main attraction. They came in many colors and were covered with gilt and silver fixtures and lined with satin. A padded kneeler always flanked the casket for friends of the deceased to stop and pray. It all seemed very Egyptian to me and I thought the dead had it cushier than the living.

Tommy Gibbons, the patriarch and neighborhood undertaker, was as Irish as they came. Dressed perpetually in a black suit, the dapper, silver haired gentleman was a crony of my Grandma Lillian, my dad's mother. She would act as a receptionist for him and mind the funeral parlor and the corpses for him while he went to Church and visited with the other turkeys in the neighborhood.

Barb and I were fascinated by this necropolis. The ramifications of death had not sunk in, we were too young. We thought the funeral displays were beautiful. We would play down the block and pick gladiolas from the funeral displays that were discarded in the alley to bring home to our mother. Sometimes we cadged a memorial ribbon or two as well. The reaction from our mother was always the same: "Get those flowers out of here," she shrieked, "I know where you found them. You got them at Gibbons." We could not understand it—we thought they were pretty, but we dutifully obeyed and tossed the flowers in the trash behind the restaurant.

My Grandma often filled in at the mortuary on Sundays and we would go down to visit her. A tiny, attractive woman with jet black hair and blue eyes who dressed smartly but conservatively, she would greet visitors, express condolences, direct the bereaved to the right room, and supervise signing of the visitors' book. My mother and Grandma Lillian were not the best of friends, having clashed when my father began dating my mother in high school. Grandma Lillian had aspirations of my dad marrying a rich heiress. He was movie star handsome and attended a toney boarding school when his father died. But Grandma Lillian's hopes were dashed when son Jack fell for Helen McMahon. My quiet, handsome, serious father was drawn to my zany, extroverted mother. She was the life of the party, always center stage, a great dancer and talker, and popular in the neighborhood. She was also smart, a good writer and did well in school. They complemented one another perfectly. My dad made his own decisions and ignored his mother, but Helen never forgot the slight.

Because of the long standing feud between my bother and my grandmother, Barb and I were deputized to bring down the Sunday dinner plate to my grandmother. My mother hated cooking and bragged about how much she hated it and how she thought she would be eating out for the rest of her life when she married a restaurant owner. I wondered, but did not ask, what my grandmother thought of the fare. Dinner usually consisted of an overcooked dried slice of pot roast or some other meat form, mashed potatoes and gravy, peas, and maybe a roll. My mom liked everything, "well done" which meant charred. My grandmother had grown up on a farm in Southern Illinois, was an excellent cook and had baked the pies and pastries for the restaurant at one time. I don't remember her complaining though. Having been widowed at a young age with two small children to raise, she was accustomed to accepting what she could get.

We jumped at the chance to go down to the funeral parlor. While our Grandma Lillian listened to Barn Dance, "hillbilly music" as my mother called it, in the back room and waited for visitors, we roamed the rooms and basement of Gibbons'. It was yet another place to explore. We were morbidly fascinated with the mortuary and the dead. Horror movies like Mr. Sardonicus and Premature Burial fueled our interest: The corpses did not frighten me, although it took some convincing to get my sister, Barb, who closed her eyes during the scary parts of movies, to peek in the caskets. We did not know anyone who had actually died and the bodies just seemed like figures from Madame Tussaud's wax museum or a William Castle horror film, not the remains of actual people. Like little Sardonicuses, we would peek in the caskets and sometimes touch the cold, hard skin. We would laugh at the clownish makeup and outlandish hairstyling that was never seen in life but adorned the departed in repose. We wrinkled our noses at the metallic formaldehyde smell that pervaded the funeral home. We pretended they woke up and told us kids to "Get out of here and let me sleep."

Since my mother and Grandma Lillian did not get along, we were also tapped to visit with our grandmother, an assignment that continued through our college years. We would spend hours at the funeral parlor, chatting with her about our childish interests and keeping her company. We were not as close to her as we were to Grandma Ma, our mother's mother, who had been our babysitter and confidante since we were born. Our mother's friction with Grandma Lillian resulted in our spending less time with her. And my mother claimed she doted on my father's sisters' children to our exclusion. I personally did not see it and actually did not care. Grandma Lillian seemed ok to me; she was no disciplinarian and let us wander at will, so I did not mind spending the time, especially if I was free to pursue my ghoulish explorations.

The funeral parlor was often the scene of Irish wakes and other shenanigans where the mourners got drunk on beer and Irish whiskey, sang songs from the auld sod, spun tales of the deceased, and got in to fights. Rumor had it that my Aunt Bernice, a notorious brawler, had duked it out with one of the bereaved (male or female? I never knew) at the funeral parlor after she'd had a few. My grandfather thereafter refused to speak to her or acknowledge her at any family events and referred to her as, "that one" followed by a "humph." There was always a spread laid out for the visitors to munch on to ease their grief. We did not partake of the feasts, however. Our mother was fanatical about our tasting food that was not refrigerated or burned. And Barb was an extremely fastidious child and would have turned her nose up at it anyway. So we smelled the food and saw the goodies and we got hungry and thirsty. We were too young for coffee and did not like the brackish brew they served to the mourners anyway. So we had to be inventive and decided to find something to make ourselves a treat.

We poked around the funeral parlor looking in drawers and sideboards, but found nothing interesting with which to work. And then I had a brainstorm. I had a chemistry set at home which I used to blow up model volcanoes and splatter the calcimine ceiling. Maybe there was something in the embalming room! We rummaged around and Eureka—we found the supply we were looking for—a big bottle of Real Lemon lemon juice. I read the directions and figured we could make some delicious lemonade for ourselves. We scoured the funeral parlor rooms for discarded sugar packets and napkins. In one of the cupboards, we found a large, empty, mason jar. We had water, so we were in business. We mixed it up and stirred it with a long metal instrument we found in a cupboard. We speculated about what the metal stir stick was used for at the funeral parlor, but figured it had been immersed in chemicals so it must be sterile. Lemon juice, about 500 sugar packets, water, a quick stir— and down the hatch, we guzzled the brew.

Barb and I declared the lemonade delicious. When we returned home after visiting our grandmother, we told my mother about our culinary skills, and she alternately laughed and choked until tears ran down her face, exclaiming, "Oh God, Oh God." Our ingenuity became the fodder for another comedy routine by my mother at her cocktail parties.

Years later, after Tommy Gibbons and my Grandma Lillian were long gone; we stood at another Gibbons' funeral parlor at my mother's wake. The grandson of Tommy Gibbons, another Tommy Gibbons, was the proprietor. We told him about visiting his grandfather's funeral parlor on West Madison Street and about the funeral displays we gave to our mom. He had never heard these tales. But when we told him about making lemonade with the embalming supplies, a look of horror crept over his face. He did not know what to make of our memories of the funny, sardonic kids we used to be. I swore I heard my mother's peals of laughter and her signature, "I thought I'd split a gut," as we told the tale and saw the look on Tommy Gibbons IV's face.

Richard and the Goldfish

I never lived my life regretting things I should have done.

It was 1955. Barbara, my younger sister, and I shared our birthday parties. We were five and seven years old. Our birthdays are one day shy of two years apart. My mother combined our parties into one big extravaganza resplendent with decorations, streamers, a cake ordered from one of the three bakeries nearby, ice cream, candy, party favors, games, prizes, Golden Books—the works. It was a lavish display not unlike Miss Havisham's wedding party the day she got jilted. And then our mother made us invite the entire neighborhood, because it wasn't "fair" to exclude anyone, even the one we despised. And, she made us invite Richard, the eight-year-old thug who pulled our hair and hit us. We definitely did not want him at the party.

"Mom, noooo. We hate that kid. He is mean. He smells and has dirty ears. He hit me."

"You cannot invite the other kids and not invite him. You will hurt his feelings." There was no arguing with Mom and her exaggerated sense of justice—Richard made the cut.

Mom needed two tables to accommodate all the guests and the loot they were getting on our birthday. Barb and I never could quite figure out why all the kids invited to our party got more presents than we did. All this on a fireman's salary? Was it misplaced charity? An attempt to feel better than other people? Competition with friends for the best kids' party? Who knows? We were the birthday girls after all. My sister and I would complain to each other about it, but never came up with an answer... "Why is she giving them more stuff than us?" We've speculated about it to this day, but we haven't come up with an answer. Was it my mother's attempt to recapture the neighborhood's faded glamour? She'd grown up in the neighborhood herself and remembered better times, school dances, dating, her wedding, happy times. She never hid her disappointment at being a fireman's wife instead of cruising through life married to a restaurateur. As it turned out, my Dad's family's business affairs were more like Bleak House than The Palmer House, played out against the backdrop of urban decay. My Dad wanted nothing to do with his relatives or the restaurant.

Mom didn't believe in waiting. When the kids arrived, girls were immediately seated at one table and boys at the other. All the treats were waiting for them and they dug in after a perfunctory "Happy Birthday to you..." the traditional wish making, and the present unwrapping. Hopped up on sugar, the kids and birthday girls adjourned to the bedroom and living room for party games and even more prizes. Jingles (Andy Devine), Wild Bill Hickok's TV sidekick smiled benevolently down on the mayhem from the bedroom wall.

I wanted a pet. When I began cursive writing I started my campaign and diligently entered every contest. Filling out box tops and entry blanks from comic books, I checked the box attesting that I had my parent's permission. I wanted to win a horse. Instead I won a dog. Mom informed the TV station, over my objections that we could not accept. I scoured the alleys for lost cats and brought them home. My mother made me give the found kittens away. The answer was always the same.

"We live in an apartment. It would be cruel to keep a pet cooped up."

Finally, we wore her down by making our case.

"The fish will be really small. She won't need a walk. We can keep her in the dining room. She won't scratch the furniture."

Mom relented about our demands for a goldfish, even though it meant cleaning out a bowl. Our purchase was approved.

Barb and I went to Neisner's, the dime store down the block, clutching our quarters and demanded assistance from the manager. This was an important purchase! Balancing our stomachs on the edge of a large tank, we netted our fish. The manager packed her up in a cardboard container filled with murky water from the tank. Barb and I agreed to name her Cleo, undoubtedly inspired by the fish in *Pinocchio*, and bought a bowl, snails, food, and ceramic castle for the new member of the family. We hurried home with our new friend. We fed her and talked to her and attributed all kinds of emotions and communication skills to the fish. She filled the bill.

When we talk about that party, Barbara remembers our mother being outraged that Richard came equipped with his own shopping bag to carry home the booty my mother laid out for the kiddies. "Was he planning this all along?" she later raged. While we played pin the tail on the donkey, blind man's bluff, and telephone, Richard—the little felon—was cleaning out the dining room, scooping up every party favor, book, plate, candy cup and noisemaker on the two tables set for the party. Once he was all packed up, he dealt us the cruelest blow of all—he fished our only pet out of her bowl and stomped Cleo into the oriental carpet.

Suddenly in the middle of Pin the Donkey, Mom, who was suspicious by nature, realized one of the revelers was missing. She told us all not to move and went looking for Richard. Mom's radar kicked in and she found him skulking down the back stairs with the bag over his shoulder like Bad Santa with his bounty. She grabbed him by the shirt collar and marched him upstairs to return all the party favors. The party guests were now clamoring for the return of their treasure and rushed my mother.

That's when we discovered the massacre—bits of goldfish and blood and bones were smeared into the carpet. In their frenzy to recover their prizes back the party guests had probably stepped on the squished remains of Cleo. It was more than we could bear. Barb and I burst into outraged tears. Our fish did not deserve this. Richard was sent home in disgrace. I promised to beat him up and my sister cried and cried.

After a sufficient period of mourning for Cleo, Barbara and I hatched our plot for revenge. Our cement backyard, where I once thought I would stable a horse, was a drop off for restaurant trash. Large steel drums of garbage were set out by my Uncle George for the pickup. The unsavory odors wafted up to the apartments— summer, winter, spring and fall. Rancid oil, reused time and time again by the restaurant staff was eventually set out for pickup. It smelled like vomit to me. It gave me a great idea.

We waited for the dust to settle and the drama to blow over, all the while conspiring to get Richard. We schemed daily about the best time to go after him. We thought about tarring and feathering him, but we had no tar. Beating him up didn't seem good enough. Then I got the brilliant idea of dousing Richard with a can of the rancid oil. I would be the executioner. Barbara, who was never the instigator but usually went along with my plans, agreed it was a good idea and a fitting revenge for our innocent fish.

We watched the trash for the can we would use for our missile. It had to be big enough to douse him and small enough for me to carry. And then, the day came! It was drizzling when dapper Uncle George, the bar manager, set out the trash. We did not want him to catch us so we waited a while. Then we descended the stairs. We picked out a juicy can of oil filled to the brim with the slime. Bits of sauerbraten, salad, potatoes, cigarette butts, and who-knows-what-else were floating on the top. It was not a small can.

We made our way across the cobblestone alley and down the block on Monroe Street to Richard's house. Richard lived in a basement apartment under the Doyle's three flat. This gave us a distinct advantage. I carried the can, careful not to spill a drop. We crept through the alley, tiptoeing on our Keds, and made our way past the raging alcoholic and local harridan, Mrs. Leyden's house. We slipped through the gangway to our positions above Richard's front door. I did not give a moment's thought about what it must be like to live in that cold, dank, basement apartment that probably flooded and smelled. I did not reflect on whether Richard envied our toys and our nice, third story apartment. He'd murdered a defenseless animal. I wanted justice.

I rang the bell. I sucked in my breath and looked at my sister. She looked pale, stared at her feet, and took a step back. The door creaked and opened. Richard squinted up at us. Staring up at the sign that proclaimed my name in lights, I dumped the whole can of oil on Richard's head. We spun on our heels and ran for it, not stopping until we made it safely home.

We remember a visit from Richard's mother, and my Mom dismissing her with "Hey, listen you, why don't you control your damn brat!" We could always count on Mom to defend us. "He killed their goldfish and tried to steal the party favors." Richard's mom stood, mouth wide open, staring blankly, barely comprehending my mother's barbs. Mom was on a roll. She slammed the heavy oak door to the back porch and laughed.

We confessed our sin.

"You did what? Oh my god, he will never get that grease out of his hair. Well, serves him right." I felt some satisfaction that I'd exacted revenge for Mom who'd put so much effort into a nice party and who'd spent the afternoon cleaning up goldfish guts off the oriental carpet.

When I was small, people would often say to me, "Girls don't do that." To which I would respond, "This girl does." Now, I think about how many shampoos and showers and scrubbings Richard had to endure and I still can't help but feel good.

Rest in Peace, little Cleo.

The King of Hearts

February was the time of year when we all had almost recovered from the hangover of Christmas and New Year's. We needed another holiday. The Presidents' Birthdays were not festive enough, and I hated cherries. Thankfully Valentine's Day was on its way. Daddy never failed to bring Mom her favorite Fannie May Pixies, flowers, and jewelry. And, there were always small satin hearts filled with Fannie May and a card for each of his daughters.

Fifth grader Anthony Lopiccolo was a lover, too. The pale skinned, freckle faced, red haired, overweight boy believed he was Casanova reincarnated. Unfortunately, the neighborhood girls thought he looked more like a great speckled egg. Nothing could stop Anthony, who made it his quest to kiss every girl in the class whether they liked it or not—he would not be deterred. He always had large amounts of cash on him; maybe this gave him unwarranted confidence with the ladies.

It didn't take long for his reputation as a serial smoocher to spread among the fourth grade girls.

"Watch out for Lopiccolo—he'll try to grab you and kiss you."

I made sure to keep my distance.

I should have thrown away his birthday party invitation when the young Lothario handed it to me, but I was never a devious kid. I showed the brightly colored "You're Invited" to Mom, and explained I had a previous engagement.

"Mom, please, I can't go—I promised Barb I'd take her to see Rodan at the Marbro."

Mom, whose sense of fairness sometimes only seemed to extend to other kids, dismissed my entreaty.

"You will hurt his feelings—you're going."

I knew I'd lost the argument before it started.

So, feet dragging, I reported for the birthday party at the Lopiccolo flat on West End.

Mrs. Lopiccolo presided over the festivities. A tall, heavy-set woman, she followed the European fashion in grooming habits; in other words, she didn't shave her legs or armpits. There was no furniture in the apartment living room or dining room; rolls of linoleum bordered the room. As guests arrived, she directed them to drop their gifts in the pile in the corner.

"Sit on the linoleum. We're redecorating."

Now when my Mom threw a party, she went all out, with party favors, cake, ice cream and treats for the guests. But these niceties were lost on Mrs. Lopiccolo. The kids played a few games and then she brought out the cake. We quickly sang a few bars of "Happy Birthday to you," Anthony blew out the candles, and the cake was whisked back to the kitchen to be cut and served.

Anthony's little brother, James, skulked in the corner, occasionally trying to grab a girl and pull her hair. We despised James. He was two years younger and in the same class as my sister, Barbara. We thought he was nasty, a budding sex maniac. While Anthony was a masher, James was more interested in the seamier side of love—he wrote obscenities on the blackboard when the nun could not see, her habit blocking her peripheral vision.

Outraged, Barb snitched on him, and James had to serve detention, while Anthony, the young romantic remained free to roam.

During the hysteria that preceded the cake and ice cream, Anthony approached me as I perched, trying to keep my balance, on the linoleum roll. True to his reputation, he whispered, "I want to show you something in the back. It's really amazing."

But I was wise to Lopiccolo and rebuffed him.

"Oh no, Anthony, I've heard all about you."

Anthony protested that I had him all wrong, and he was really trying to show me a toy, then a game, then kittens; nothing worked. He quickly lost interest when Mrs. Lopiccolo returned with the plates of cake and ice cream.

"Birthday boy, get over here. You're first."

I silently prayed that Mom would show up soon to pick me up, and she finally did, but we could not escape yet. Mrs. Lopiccolo, who towered over my mother, cornered Mom in the doorway, to tell her about her redecorating plans. Trapped under Mrs. L's armpit, Mom tried to squirm her way out but she was trapped. Her face grew redder and redder.

I chuckled when we finally walked out on the stoop and Mom exhaled.

"Phew, I don't think that woman uses deodorant." "Ha, serves you right, Mom. You made me go."

Mom went on. "What a dump—they have more money than sense."

Finally, I got my point across. "Anthony tried to KISS me!"

"Kiss you? What? Oh no—you're never going there again."

But love was all around us. In the 1950s and early 1960s, St. Mel Holy-Ghost School sponsored an endless onslaught of charitable giving campaigns from September when we walked through the doors of the venerable institution until June when we ran frantically from the hallowed halls to our summer months of freedom.

There was never a dull moment at St. Mel-Holy Ghost School. Every date in the liturgical calendar was a golden opportunity to raise money for the "poor starving children in other countries." I had to hand it to the nuns—they were pretty clever. Every holy day and holiday, they had a gimmick to appeal to our consciences, our concern for our fellow man, and our charity. And, despite all evidence to the contrary, those nuns were successful in making us believe there was someone less fortunate than ourselves. Quite a feat, considering we were living in a slum, a neighborhood to which urban renewal would never come.

Valentine's Day was yet another occasion for this magic act. St. Mel Church itself was monumental, built by the community in 1910 and designed after the Romanesque style of architecture; it boasted the best Carrera marble of Italy and finest acoustical design. It accommodated 1250 people and they always packed the house.

Every year, on the Sunday before St. Valentine's Day, just after the Gospel was read, the parish priest would cede his time in the pulpit, time usually devoted to very important exhortations to repent or be cast into hellfire, to the Maryknoll missionary priest.

I liked this part of the Mass—we got to get off the kneelers and sit down, so I'd listen to anything just to get a break. The missionary courted us with tales of exotic places, of deepest Africa, of lions, rhinos, giraffes, elephants and the Serengeti—and the little children who had no shoes, no food, no schools, no medical care, and who would never know God and be stuck in Limbo unless we helped. He told us we could change the lives of these poor little children.

So wooed by a pitch delivered at the 9 a.m. Sunday Children's Mass by the missionary priest, we were suddenly transformed from the urchins who hung out every day at the Off the Street Club to benefactors of children in foreign lands—donors whose largesse and beneficence would bring the little children to God.

And so it was this St. Valentine's Day. Another contest was announced, another chance for Catholic school kids to mitigate their guilt for having it so good. Sister Veronica Ann made the announcement over the P.A. This year, the school would crown a King and Queen of Hearts. Children would be permitted to purchase hearts made of construction paper for 10 cents a pop and make crowns with the hearts and materials provided in the classroom. The girl and boy who donated the most money and had the largest crowns would be anointed the King and Queen of Hearts.

I had to admit—this contest seemed like a stretch to me. I wished them luck but I was skeptical of its success, especially when our Principal emphasized that the hearts should be purchased with money that we earned all by ourselves. How was I going to do that—I was just ten! I only had $1 that I got from Gramps every week and there was no way I was skipping my customary Saturday at the movies to buy some crummy hearts. I decided to hit Mom up for the extra cash, but Mom was not buying it either.

"You want money for what? Hearts made out of construction paper? What are they going to come up with next? Last week, it was a greasy donut drive. I've still got seven boxes of those donuts sitting here—no one will touch them. You know I only buy Burny Brothers baked goods. And the week before that it was the subscription drive for the New World."

Now Mom was feeling the pinch after the Christmas bills rolled it and was not feeling the love. But I pressed her to dig deep.

"Mom, I will be humiliated if I don't buy some. I will be the only kid in class without a crown. Come on, please."

Just then, Daddy walked in on this exchange.

"Does Sister Mary Holy Water want more money from us?" Dad called all the nuns "Sister Mary Holy Water."

I patiently explained the latest promotion to Daddy, whose expression grew more and more skeptical with each word I spoke.

"That sounds stupid."

"Dad, please, we'll be EMBARRASSED."

That clinched it. Dad would not let us be shamed in front of the class. He reached in his pocket and pulled out his money clip, peeling off two dollars.

"Alight, here, a buck a piece—but that's it! What a racket."

The next day Barb and I returned to school, weighed down, at Mom's insistence, with Valentines for every kid in the class—even Lopiccolo and Timothy Donahue, who tried to give us ringworm. Clutching the dollars Dad gave us, we were feeling secure. We could buy some hearts and no teacher would bug us about it. When we walked through the door, a frenzy of kids in hat crowns, hopped up on sugar hearts, ran and skipped down the hall.

Then a wondrous sight greeted me. Parading the halls with a crown that looked like a Native American war bonnet was Cupid himself, the Chairman of Love, Anthony Lopiccolo. The crown he wore trailed several feet behind his round little body and kids laughed and followed him like he was we the Pied Piper, trying their best to step on the ends.

I poked Barb.

"He must have spent 20 bucks on that thing."

Ever the style maven, Barb dismissed Anthony with a sniff.

"It's gross."

Anthony did not care what we thought. He was in his glory that Valentine's Day when he was crowned the King of Hearts of St. Mel's School in recognition of his generous contribution to the missions. Unfortunately, the title did not change his luck with the girls – they still ran away, squealing, when he tried to grab them and kiss them.

Ever the Romeo, Anthony continued to seek love in vain. That is, until one day when I saw him walking Theresa, our blind classmate, home from school, carrying the large binders that held her Braille books. The next day the girls pulled her aside to fill her in.

"Theresa, we saw you walking with Anthony yesterday. He is icky. He tries to kiss all the girls."

"Oh, I know, he is just trying to be nice."

"But Theresa, he is fat and he has red hair and freckles."

Theresa stopped us dead.

"I'm blind. I don't care what he looks like. He is nice to me."

She had us there. Anthony would no longer go looking for love in all the wrong places. I realized that Theresa had the ability to discover something deeper in him than we had been willing or able to. Cupid had struck true with someone who saw straight into the heart of the King of Hearts.

The Matriarch
of Madison Street

Bethlehem on Madison Street

Staring at the ceiling didn't help. I tried lying very still under the magenta colored silky down comforter, but it was no good. I rubbed my feet on the sheets and tossed around. Counting sheep didn't work. Finally, I whispered to Barb.

"Still awake?"

"Yes, I can't sleep."

"Me neither"

Although we usually pushed our bedtimes out as late as we could, Christmas Eve was different. We'd donned our nightgowns without an argument and gone to bed early, hoping that we would fall asleep, wake up and it would be Christmas Day. But our little girl excitement about the holiday and the gifts and visiting with family was proving to be too much. We were both wide awake and Christmas Day wasn't arriving any sooner. From the living room, we heard the muted sounds of Rosemary Clooney's Christmas carols coming from the television that Mom left on to keep her company when Daddy was at the firehouse. Mom dozed on the couch; between the Coke and the M &Ms, she never slept well when Daddy was not home.

Madison Street was quiet; a heavy, blowing snowfall muffled the sounds of the streetcar on its way to the barn. Occasionally a car would drive by—maybe a fireman or policeman taking a few hours off to spend time with his kids? Last minute shoppers had carted their packages home hours ago. The shops and restaurants along our street always closed early so that the employees could spend Christmas Eve with their families.

BZZZZZZZZZZ! The buzzer squawked announcing a visitor. I heard Mom mumble, "Who the heck is that now?" and shuffle down the long hall to the intercom.

"Who's there?" Mom's standard greeting was to the point.

"Who? I can't hear you. Noreen?"

By then we'd snuck out of bed. Barb and I peered down the hall, the thoroughfare that connected the rooms in our apartment. Mom was in her nightgown, robe and slippers, hair in pin curls. She'd lit a cigarette on her way down the hall. She took a drag, pausing for a moment, and then yelled back in the intercom.

"Noreen, c'mon up. I am going to buzz you in."

Mom hit the intercom buzzer that opened the heavy oak door in the tiled entry way to our apartments. She walked to the front door and opened it. By then we weren't hiding—we wanted to know what was up. We followed her to the door and waited to see who the nocturnal visitor was. Mom leaned over the railing at the top of the stairs. This was our extra security system. If we bent over the banister at just the right angle, we could see people coming up the stairs before they saw us, giving us plenty of time to run in and slam the front door before they reached the top. Mom often said, "If anyone wants to climb those three flights of stairs and steal something from this dump, they can have it." The heavy oak door of our apartment was impregnable and we always felt safe on the third floor.

Slowly, breathing heavily, holding on to the banister for support, a tall, thin woman holding a paper sack in one hand ascended the stairs. In the other, she held the hand of a little girl, smaller than Barb or me, but not a toddler. Each step the woman took seemed more difficult for her. When she got to the second story landing, where Mom could see her better, Mom hurried down the stairs to help her. Mom took the child's hand and the paper sack and led them up the stairs to our apartment.

Noreen stood in the entry way, perspiring, near the big walnut desk that held the telephone and served as a reception area for our guests. Her coat was a thin, worn, loden green cloth coat, not much protection from the bleak Chicago winter outside. She had no gloves or boots, and a rayon scarf was tied over her head and knotted at the chin. Her daughter was dressed in warmer clothes, a snowsuit, mittens and boots. The little girl yawned and leaned against her mother. Noreen hesitated, embarrassed.

"I don't want to get your floors wet."

Mom replied, "Aw, don't worry about this dump. Come on in. Stand on this rug while I get you some slippers. Anita, go get the little girl—what's your name?—a pair of your slippers. I'm sorry, what's your name, Honey? Christine? Oh that's pretty. A pretty name for a pretty girl. Your nickname is Cookie. You're my Christmas Cookie."

I ran to the bedroom closet and pulled out a pair of my old slippers, Chinese silk backless beauties with a rose embroidered across the toes that I had saved long after I grew out of them. Gram and Gramps had purchased them for me when we visited San Francisco and I could not let them go. I had huge feet that grew quickly for a small girl and, pretty soon after I bought them, my heels were hanging off the back of the slippers, so I put them away in the closet. *These are too big, but maybe we can stuff them with toilet paper.*

By the time I came back with the slippers, Mom had ushered our visitors into the living room, hung their coats in the bathroom, and was offering them goodies.

"Do you want a Coke? How about some Christmas candy? Some chips? Dip?"

Mom was no cook, but she always had a great supply of snacks available. Noreen shook her head and declined softly.

"No, thank you, Helen. We're fine."

It was pretty clear they weren't. The entry hall was dark but now I could see Noreen in a better light. She was tall, very frail, and seemed timid. Her hair was a mousy brown—once it must have been much lighter, and the hairstyle was dated, like the styles I saw in Mom's old photos from the 1940s. I thought she had a nice face, kind, with high cheekbones and she could have been attractive, but she was so slight. That was saying something since our Mom was always skinny and prided herself on her petite frame. Noreen wheezed and coughed, but her breathing seemed less labored now that she was resting on our sofa. Her daughter, cheeks still rosy from the cold outside, curled up in the corner and promptly fell asleep, smiling, wearing my slippers. I poked Barb and gave her a knowing look and nodded. Mom won't even let us sit on that sofa. She must like this woman. Some old friend? No, she's too young. She looks familiar, though. She seems to know me.

Mom left us for a few minutes while she went to the kitchen to heat some coffee—she could drink coffee night or day. Noreen smiled at Barb and me.

"You girls have gotten so big. Do you remember me? I used to play with you and read you stories sometimes."

Then I recognized her. And I felt shocked and sad. Noreen lived in the apartment next door when Barb and I were tots. She was a teenager then and had some kind of live in arrangement with the apartment dwellers that had two small children. Even though I was quite young, I remember wondering why she wasn't in school like my babysitters, and why she didn't live with her parents. I asked Mom one time and she said that Noreen's parents were "drinkers and couldn't take care of her" and that she'd been passed around to different relatives who did not want her. Noreen was always nice to Barb and me, and when she was not working for the couple, she'd play games with us or read to us on the back porch or on the landing in between the two apartments. Mom always had a soft spot for any person down on their luck, and she took a special interest in the young woman, giving her clothes and slipping her money sometimes, when she could afford to.

Mom came back in the living room with the coffee and suddenly we were on her radar again.

"Why are you two up? Get back in bed—NOW!"

We wanted to hear Noreen's story, too, and why she was at our house on Christmas Eve instead of her own, but that was not going to happen. Mom shooed us out of the living room and back to our bedroom. It didn't occur to me then but she wanted to protect Noreen's privacy and her feelings. We would not hear her story until later.

I strained to hear what they were saying but the walls were thick and I couldn't hear anything clearly without getting out of bed. Mom had x-ray vision and she would know that I got up so I figured it was pointless. Then Barb and I saw her walk down the hall and come back with a nightgown, blankets and pillows.

I guessed that Noreen and Cookie would be staying the night. That was no surprise. We'd had many visitors staying with us over the years. Mom always found the room. We became aware of hushed conversations over the years between Mom and Dad. Someone was in trouble, someone needed money or a place to stay—folks knew they could turn to Mom. Daddy might protest a bit—"Helen, I can't afford it. I'm busting my butt now"—but he always came through and his second job at Bantam Books down by the Chicago River helped bail out those in need. I don't think my parents ever got the "loans" paid back and they never asked for repayment. Mom had time for everyone. All the down-on-their-luck men who lived in the flophouses along Skid row and haunted the bus stops in the Loop knew her by name. They'd wave and call out, "Helen!" and for a moment a smile would come over their faces. She knew all their stories; she loved to talk and always had a few bucks for every one of them. It made her feel good to give.

I was drifting back to sleep when a thought alarmed me—we had no presents for Cookie! I panicked. What would we do? It was too late to go shopping; the stores had closed hours before.

Barb must have had the same thought, too, because she whispered, "Maybe we could give her some of our presents."

"Barb, that's a great idea. Good thinking. But what should we give her? We don't know what's in the boxes. They're wrapped."

I pondered this dilemma for a moment and then had a brainstorm.

"OK, listen, how about this? We sneak in before Mom gets up and rip the tags off the presents and give them to Cookie." Barb agreed this sounded like a good plan.

"You know, Aunt Camille always gives us a nightgown or pajamas, and that little girl has no pajamas. We've got a bunch. Mine would be too big for her, so you get your box from Aunt

Camille and rip off the tag. Grandma Lillian always gives me a book, so I will give her mine. But ya know, those aren't very fun presents."

Barb spoke softly, "What about a game? We always get a game or two for Christmas. There has to be a game under the Christmas tree. Those Milton Bradley games are all the same shape. We'll be able to find it. She doesn't have any toys with her, so she'll need a game."

"Yes, that's it. Now, listen. If you wake up first, wake me up, and if I do I will wake you up. We are going to have to be really, really quiet. Mom won't hear us because she likes to sleep late, but Noreen and her little girl might wake up. We don't want them to see us—that would spoil the surprise."

Barb and I were soon off to sleep. We could rest easy now that we had Christmas presents for Cookie covered. A few times I was roused and thought I heard coughing, but went right back to sleep.

Next morning we were up early. We dressed in our matching quilted robes, but left our slippers off, and tiptoed down the hall to our living room. Noreen was on one sofa, in one of Mom's best nightgowns; while Cookie lay on the other sofa in exactly the same spot she had fallen asleep. Someone had covered her with a hand knit baby blanket. Mom probably. Barb, the artist, had cleverly brought her supplies—a little round edged pair of scissors for cutting off the gift tags, and a colored pencil for printing Cookie's name on the newly assigned boxes. We worked quickly in silence. We located the boxes and Barb cut off the gift tags and shoved them in the pocket of her robe. I had the best printing, so I wrote the new greetings right on the paper.

"Merry Christmas, Cookie, from Santa."

I didn't believe in Santa, although I still made my annual trip to Madigan's Department store to tell him what I wanted, but this is what Mom and Dad always wrote on our presents so I thought I would do the same. Cookie was pretty young and I bet she would not recognize my handwriting.

"Let's go back to bed. We'll have to wait until they get up or we'll blow it."

Barb crawled in my twin bed while we waited for what seemed like forever for the rest of the household to get up. Finally, the Babies, Donna and Jackie, started to make some racket in the back bedroom and I heard my mom moving around in the kitchen, making more coffee in the old aluminum percolator she used every day, and dialing someone on the telephone. Nothing out of the ordinary there. Mom was always on the phone.

"It's safe. Let's get up."

We ran into the living room, festooned with Mom's decorations, tinseled tree—Daddy's pride and joy, mantel covered with ceramic holiday figures rubbing elbows with the oriental knickknacks Mom collected then, and gas fake fireplace aglow. It was a glorious scene. The Babies were all over the presents and started tearing the gift wrap off anything they could reach. Noreen and Cookie gazed from the sidelines, seeming a bit overwhelmed.

Then Mom was on the scene, putting a halt to the mayhem.

"Hold on. Your father is on his way. He has a few hours off today and he wants to see you unwrap your gifts."

"Awww, Mom. He won't be home for hours. Can't we open some, puh-leeze?

Mom caved in—it was an unusual Christmas anyway. "OK, but you have to say some of the big ones. He'll be disappointed if he doesn't get to watch."

This gave me my opportunity. I poked Barb and we grabbed the presents we'd regifted for Cookie. The little girl had slid off the couch where she slept and was snuggled close to her mother now. We marched up to her and, unceremoniously, presented her with the boxes.

"Here, Cookie. Santa left these for you."

The little girl popped off the sofa, still wearing my slippers and reached for the gifts.

Noreen protested quietly to Mom, "Oh no, please, you've done enough for us." She bit her lip and looked as if she might cry.

Mom spoke up, "This is their idea; I didn't know anything about it." But we could tell she was pleased with her girls.

While the Babies tried to derail the Lionel train set up under the tree—a gift from Gramps—we all snacked on Pillsbury cinnamon rolls straight from a tube. Mom had managed not to burn them this time and the spirals, dripping with thick, sugary frosting tasted pretty good with the Fannie Mae chocolate Santas from our stockings. Barb and I set up what turned out to be a Captain Kangaroo game. I read the instructions to Barb and Cookie and we all played a few rounds.

Mom turned serious for a moment.

"You girls get dressed. Father Shaughnessy and Father Riordan are coming over."

We hurried to the bathroom to wash up and then to our bedroom to get dressed. I wondered what this was all about. Mom was pretty friendly with all the priests and nuns in our parish but they usually only came to the house on special occasions like Holy Communions, weddings, and to give Extreme Unction. I thought they'd be busy saying Christmas Mass or something. Wasn't this one of their big days?

Now this was long before anyone thought of the War on Poverty and safety nets for women and children in need just did not exist. Many destitute mothers and children fell through the cracks in those days. Jobs were few and opportunities very limited for women. Many would turn to their families—but what if there was no family? We knew Mom was there for anyone who told her they needed help. She loved St. Mel–Holy Ghost Church. She grew up here and was married in this Church. She supported St. Mel's and the Church was there to back her up. I realized the early phone call must have been to the priests who ministered to our parishioners.

The doorbell rang again and Mom went to welcome the two priests. Father Shaughnessy greeted us and Father Riordan patted me on the head. She offered them coffee and Pillsbury rolls, but they declined. They were still on call to say Mass. Father Shaughnessy, the young energetic, activist priest who headed all the youth programs in the neighborhood, hair prematurely thinning, looked dapper in his Roman collar and black suit. He removed his fedora as he stepped in the door. Father Riordan accompanied him. Wire rimmed glasses, dark hair graying at the temples; he was the more mature of the two. Mom saw the older priest as a father figure; he'd married Mom and Dad and baptized me and Mom often turned to him for counsel. She introduced them to Noreen and Cookie and then shooed us out of the living room.

"OK, you two, get outta here, go play with your presents or something. I need to talk with Father Shaughnessy and Father Riordan."

We knew better than to argue. This order from Mom signaled adult conversation and we'd better move it.

We overheard some of the conversation from the front bedroom. Mom telling the priests about how she knew Noreen, how Noreen had been baptized Catholic, but not raised in the Church, something about a deadbeat husband and nowhere to go, and how she needed their help. Noreen's faith did not matter to the priests; they were here to offer aid. I thought I heard someone crying very softly. Then just as quickly, the priests were off, back to their holiday duties at the Church, but not before they gave us all a blessing and wished us a "Happy, Holy Christmas." Father Shaughnessy said he'd be back a little later to pick up Noreen and Cookie.

Mom went to work; she requisitioned a small suitcase from the hall closet where all the large items, including a stove, were stored. Rummaging through closets and drawers, she pulled blouses, sweaters, skirts, stockings, a hat and gloves for Noreen. It was a challenge since Noreen was much taller than Mom and nearly gaunt, but Mom found some clothing that would work. She dug through the cedar chest and located some pants, skirts, and blouses I had grown out of for Cookie. She'd been planning to pack them up and send them to my cousin Kim; Barb was so petite; it would be years before they would fit her. And then Mom pulled a mouton lamb fur coat from the closet.

Noreen protested, "No, no. I can't accept that, Helen. Your fur coat."

"Take it—it's cold out there and I've been after Jack to buy me a mink. Now he'll have to." Mom laughed, but it would be many years before she got her mink.

It seemed like he'd just left, but the buzzer rang, and Father Shaughnessy was buzzed up again. His big black, donated Cadillac was parked at the curb downstairs in front of Solick's Restaurant. One of the perks for a lifetime of service, his Caddy was a shuttle bus for anyone who needed a ride. He picked up the suitcase in one hand and carried Cookie in his other arm downstairs to the car. Noreen stopped for a moment on the landing and gave me and Barb a kiss on our cheeks. Then Mom walked Noreen downstairs and we watched Mom as she hugged Noreen and waved goodbye as they drove off with Father Shaughnessy.

The decorated lampposts and the Solick's restaurant sign were so glittery and festive. The neon Christmas trees decorating the sign that blinked by turns in a row made it seem like an enchanted forest. But that morning, the holiday trimmings seemed to highlight the fantasy world we lived in, and even to my child's eyes, were a stark contrast to the harsh reality that had entered our safe house that Christmas Eve.

When Mom came back upstairs we badgered her with questions.

"Are they coming back? Where did they go? Where is Father Shaughnessy taking them? Are they going to have dinner with us?"

Then Mom told us that Noreen and Cookie would not be coming back soon. She said Noreen was very sick and had to go to the hospital. "TB", she whispered. The disease was dreaded, especially among those of Irish descent. Mom had many relatives who'd succumbed to tuberculosis and she was paranoid every time we caught cold even though we insisted our Bohemian blood would save us.

"Noreen'll be away for a long time. Father Shaughnessy and Father Riordan found some nice people who have a lot of kids and they are going to take care of Cookie while her Mom is getting well."

"But what about her dad?"

"Cookie's dad was not nice to them. He hurt them."

We couldn't imagine it—Daddy and Grandpa treated us like little princesses, and never got angry with us.

"Girls, be thankful for what you have. Noreen had had a very hard life. She lived with one family after another who did not want her after her parents took off. She got married young—don't you ever do that—and the man was mean to her and her daughter. Then she ran away from him, but she's been sick. She told me she was just walking the street last night in the snow, no money and no food, and then she saw our lights on and rang the bell. Thank God she did."

We nodded our heads in agreement although we did not completely understand the gravity of Noreen's situation. Then Mom said, "I was so proud of you, giving Cookie your presents. You are my stars!" Praise from Mom was the best present of all.

Later Daddy would come home and watch us open some gifts while he grabbed something to eat and then went back to fight the inevitable holiday fires. Gram and Gramps would come by and Gram would cook a feast for us all to eat together. Gramps would slip us a "sawbuck" when he thought no one was looking. Barb and I would play with our toys until we got sick of them. The Babies would get into all our gifts and rip up more wrapping paper, making a mess of the living room, and Mom would laugh. A pageant of Aunts and uncles, cousins and friends would stop by our apartment with gifts to wish us Merry Christmas and Happy New Year. But somehow I knew this holiday was even more special and that I was a very lucky girl.

Years later we moved from our beloved West Garfield neighborhood to a small bungalow on the Northwest Side. I was in a Catholic girls' high school now and had grown at least a foot. Barb was a freshman at the same high school. Donna and Jackie went to the local parochial school and Mom had gone back to work. It was a nice Saturday in spring; the trees were budding and my allergies were kicking in. The doorbell rang; I thought it might be the postman and ran to see if my new Beatles magazine had come in the mail.

A young, nice-looking woman holding a baby boy stood on the stoop. A girl stood next to her.

"Are you Anita? Oh my gosh—you've grown so much. Is Helen—your Mom—home?"

By then Mom was behind me. "Noreen, is that you? Oh you look great! Is this your baby? He's beautiful. Look how big he is! How old is he? Hi, sweetie. Is this Cookie? You've grown up! What grade are you in now?"

The young family was ushered into our tiny bungalow living room and provided with Mom's favorite treats for guests— Coke, potato chips, and onion dip. Mom and Noreen chatted and Noreen caught Mom up on her life after she left us that Christmas Day many years before.

She said she'd been very ill and was hospitalized for a long time. Father Shaughnessy and Father Riordan arranged for her care at no charge. She'd lost a lung. While she was in the sanitarium, a very nice family cared for Cookie, and when Noreen came out, they helped her get on her feet. It was this couple who introduced her to a cousin, a solid, considerate young man who became her second husband, the father of the new baby.

"He's an engineer. We have a nice house now and he loves Cookie. I am happy, Helen. I bumped into someone from the West Side last week and they said you'd moved up here, so I thought I'd take a chance and see if you were home. I don't feel like I ever thanked you enough. I don't know what would have happened to me if you hadn't taken me in that night."

"I'm just happy to hear everything worked out for you and Cookie, Noreen. I am glad to see you healthy again. I've thought of you many times and prayed for you."

"Helen, I will never forget you or your girls and what you did for me. You changed my life. Your apartment was like Bethlehem on Madison Street that Christmas Eve."

Some Assembly Required

必要ないくつかのアセンブ

Christmas holidays at my apartment on Madison Street resembled the excess of the scene in *A Christmas Carol* when the Spirit of Christmas Present makes his appearance. Thanks to my mother and her holiday zeal, a cornucopia of Christmas candy, toys, games and food materialized in our living room every year.

Sweets of every conceivable variety appeared in dishes around the room. One kind of chocolate was never enough. My mother had a formidable sweet tooth. She even liked candy we hated, and bought it all. She lived the rest of the year on M&Ms, Coca Cola and cigs, supplementing her diet with barbeque potato chips for fiber. As the Christmas holidays approached, the every growing mountain of candy came as no surprise to us—kids who knew there might not be milk in the fridge, but there would always be a six pack of Coke. Fannie May, Dutch Mill, Brach's mints, solid chocolate Santas, ribbon candy and candy canes—we had it all.

The living room was decorated to the nines. A wreath with, very fittingly, a stuffed Santa Claus doll toasting us with a Coke adorned the mantel over the fireplace. Syrupy, dark, bubbly Coke was always the drink of choice in our house. The mantel hosted Santa's sleigh and reindeer, a papier mache display made by the disabled kids at my grandmother's school, Nativity scenes, angels, elves, candles, and other Christmas figurines. It was a bright, festive crowd up there.

The Christmas tree was my father, Jack's, bailiwick and work of art. My dad grew up in the apartment we lived in and he took special pride in selecting and decorating the tree. A type A personality if ever there was one, Daddy would only agree to trees purchased from Amling's Nursery. The tree had to be tall to fit the room. The ceilings in the living room were 12 feet with crown molding. The tree also had to be fresh and perfectly symmetrical with no bare branches or bare spots. It had to be tall enough so that the star touched the ceiling. We would accompany my dad when he selected the tree. He examined every candidate, until he found THE perfect tree. Of course—we always agreed with his choice. When the tree came home, it was immediately placed in the tree stand and faithfully watered it to keep it looking good. The tree was up and decorated well before Christmas and came down promptly on the Feast of the Epiphany.

When the tree's branches had relaxed sufficiently, my dad began the meticulous process of decorating the tree. First the lights went on, followed by the tinsel. He would hang the leaden tinsel strand by strand, branch by branch, starting from the trunk of the tree out to the tip of the branch until each was full. Finally, hundreds of glass ornaments, fantastic in their design, were hung. The glass star topped the tree and Dad's masterpiece was complete!

Our anticipation of the Christmas gala began as soon as we took off our Halloween costumes. Thanksgiving, after all, did not include candy or toys, and did not count as a real holiday. My Mother started with the Christmas buildup right after Halloween and even got a small Christmas tree for my younger siblings; that is, until she had to perform triage removing the shards when toddler Donna crawled up and took a bite out of an appealing glass ornament. We lived on the big commercial street in the neighborhood and we watched as merchants decorated their windows with holiday scenes, soaped the glass to resemble snow and promoted Christmas gift buying. Even the street lamps were decorated every year, with wreaths and ornaments, and I thought they added a special touch as we viewed them from our third story perch.

Barb and I attended the local parochial school, St. Mel–Holy Ghost School, and we were steeped in the liturgy of the Catholic Church and the Latin Mass. The liturgical calendar was a great build up for the holiday. From the beginning of Advent on, we prepared for the birth of the Baby Jesus by stocking larder. Even as a child, the irony was not lost on me. Jesus in a stable was a reason for us to load up on the goodies.

My parents filled the back bedroom closet with gifts for the Kids (as Barb and I were called) and the Babies (as my toddler younger sister, Donna, and brother, Jackie, were dubbed.) The Parents removed the door knob so we couldn't peek at the booty, but I quickly figured out how to pick the lock with a screwdriver. Not wanting to spoil all the surprises, I only opened the door briefly so that Barb and I could do a quick check to make sure they had not forgotten anything we REALLY wanted.

I knew then that Helen was not just buying those toys for us and that many of the gifts would soon be packed up and make their way west to Washington State where my mother's sister, Alice, and her brood lived. I had noticed early on that if I lost interest in a toy or game, it disappeared—boxed up and sent to Alice's for one of our 10 cousins to enjoy. This didn't seem at all strange at the time. There were a lot of those kids and not a lot of money to go around, and, of course, my mother was well known for her generosity. If I inquired about what happened with a missing toy, she responded with, "You weren't playing with that thing any way; I sent it to Alice's kids." And that was that.

By 1957 at age nine, I definitely did not believe in Santa any more, if I ever really had. I know I continued to play the game for a while, cognizant that with an admission of disbelief came an instant reduction in the gift inventory. But Barb was seven and on the cusp, and she still wanted to believe. And I had a secret—I was a child atheist. This abandonment of faith was founded in two incidents—concluding that Peter Pan was not real and rejecting religion completely after my first Communion when I got a host stuck in my throat.

Peter Pan was my childhood idol. I wanted to be him. I insisted on being Peter Pan for the kindergarten Halloween party even though he was a boy. I thrilled at his exploits when I saw the Disney movie with my father at the Paradise Theater. My dad bought a Peter Pan hat for me and a Tinkerbell wand for Barb, who was sick with pneumonia. I loved the wild child who ran free, fought with pirates, could fly, and had no adult supervision. I could not relate to Wendy at all. Egged on by my Mother's teenage cousins, who were my babysitters when my parents went out nightclubbing, I waited at the window and called every night for Peter to come and take me to Neverland. I sang the song from the Disney movie and jumped off the bed thousands of times in an attempt to fly. Eventually, my babysitters' sniggering and the fact that Peter was a no show sunk it. It was all a fairy tale.

The gory statues in Church had bothered me for some time and I mused why people would want to scare little children with depictions of torture. But the host adventure was the one incident that put me over the edge. In those days, fasting for 24 hours was required before you received the host, a small, dry, sharp, tasteless disc that was supposed to be the Body of Jesus Christ through the Miracle of Transubstantiation. One Sunday, after I received Communion, the darned host lodged in my throat. Since I hadn't eaten or drunk anything since Saturday, I could not swallow it or move it with my tongue which was as dry as #180 fine grade sandpaper.

Kneeling in the pew, I glanced furtively to see if anyone was looking, and when I saw the coast was clear, risking eternal damnation, jammed the host down my throat with my finger. Nothing happened. The child skeptic in me was born. The Heavens did not open up and I did not go to Hell. I reasoned then that no sensible God would send a small child to Hell for preventing themselves from choking, so the whole story must be a fabrication. I also figured I better not let anyone know I had figured this out or I would be in big trouble.

So it wasn't surprising that Santa got the boot. Being the eldest gave me an edge, and it wasn't too long before I connected the dots about old St. Nick. Simple powers of observation. I recorded the bags and boxes hustled up the back stairs and into the closet by my parents. I checked out the dimensions of the chimney and concluded no fat guy was going to make it through that narrow hole, much less the flue. I scrutinized the spirit gum on the old man's nylon beard at Madigan's Department Store. No one had to tell me this was a hoax. It was a good hoax though, and I decided it was in my best interests to play along.

But 1957 proved to be the end of the line for me. After this year, I could no longer keep up the ruse. 1957 was also the year my mother discovered catalog shopping. She shared the catalogs and Barb and I poured over the colored ads, fantasizing about all the treasures that could be ordered at such marvelous savings. "RETAIL— WHOLESALE—YOUR PRICE!" the advertising screamed. By the fourth grade, I could do the math and shared the exciting results with Barb. We agreed our parents could buy us many more toys and games for the same investment they had previously made. We drafted our lists and passed them on to my mother.

Since my dad was a young Chicago fireman, the holidays were a busy time and meant grueling hard work for him. He often worked for days without a break or sleep, sustained on donuts and coffee from the Salvation Army. He fought fires in subzero weather in the ice and snow while people burned their homes down with candles on Christmas trees, faulty lights, and dinners forgotten in the oven while they tied one on. This Christmas was no exception. My dad had been up for several days without sleep when he arrived home on Christmas Eve. It was the practice to let the firemen who worked on Christmas go home for a few hours to see their families and catch some sleep and a meal.

But when my dad arrived, my mom sprung it on him. His work was not done. There, waiting for him, were dozens of toys purchased through the catalog that needed assembly. Now, my dad was not a patient man except with us kids. His perfectionism dominated his personality. He was also a pragmatic person, and knowing his limitations, he did little around the house. If something needed fixing, he instructed my Mother to "pay somebody." My sympathy was with my dad. He worked another job on his days off so the last thing he wanted to do when he came home was to work on home repairs. And putting toys with small pieces together was way out of his comfort zone.

I will say he gave it his best 20 minute shot before he blew his stack, but the lack of sleep and physical exhaustion got the best of even my stoic Dad. As he fumbled with the small parts, his face got redder and redder; "Goddammit, Helen—why did you buy this shit anyway!" he exploded. The expletives began to flow. I thought he would foam at the mouth. He dumped the pieces of a playhouse on the living room floor, and threw in the towel. "I am beat and I am going to bed." Helen wailed like a banshee, "You can't—the babies will wake up and they won't have any presents!" Screaming ensued but in the end my dad hit the sack for some much needed rest.

Helen panicked. She was a creative person, but there was too much to do before the Babies woke up. Conspiratorially, she brought me and my sister, Barb, to the dining room to enlist our help. "We'll have to put the toys together," she said. Then, looking down at Barb, she bluntly stated, "Well, you didn't believe in HIM anymore any way, did you?" Barb meekly sputtered, "Well, no, I guess not." She looked crestfallen for a brief moment and then, collecting herself said, "No, I can help, too."

So the three of us turned the living room into Santa's workshop. Barb and I in pin curls and pajamas, put toy after toy together. Amazing, since we had no prior mechanical experience, the tools were Scotch tape, a screwdriver and scissors, and the instructions were not in English. I figured that since we prayed in Latin in Church every day, I had it wired. Unfortunately, Japanese is not a romance language. I could decipher that Tab AA went into Slot AA, but that was as far as my classical language skills were taking me that night. A particularly fiendish challenge was a tiny cardboard chest of drawers for a doll. Barb and I agreed the Babies would never know the difference if it wasn't quite right and the objective was to get it together by morning. So we cut and taped and shoved pieces together until something like a chest of drawers emerged from the chaos. We agreed that if it fell apart we could fix it later.

We worked until the wee hours, jacked up on candy and the cookies we were going to leave for Santa. What the heck, we figured, we were Santa. Finally, we had all the toys set up under the tree. In the process, we had seen all our gifts, too. As we assembled our own toys, our mother said, "Oh yeah, this is for you." We did not care that the surprise was spoiled. We had graduated. We felt like adults, we were the big kids, we were our mother's confidantes and we helped our dad.

The Babies woke up next morning and found their toys, not a bunch of small pieces littered on a living room floor. Years later, my sister Donna still had the little doll chest, but she used it to store socks and underwear. It was still taped together, leaning slightly, the drawers sticking when you tried to open them. No one had ever bothered to put it together correctly, but it never fell apart, a kind of crazy, tiny cabinet of Dr. Caligari testament to our childhood ingenuity.

Helen the Hotline

I rode the rotor wheel 'round and 'round, yelling, "Faster, faster!" to Barb who was at the helm, pushing the wheel while I clung to the metal handle bar, bracing my feet against the round iron base so I wouldn't fly off. I loved thrill rides and to keep myself from vomiting, I kept my eyes on my Mom, returning again and again to my focal point like a ballerina doing a pirouette.

Barb and I played at this little playground near the public school. She had a friend who lived on the next block and we would meet up there. We passed the school, never failing to chant, "Tilton, T, Tilton, T, Tilton Penitentiary." Usually Barb and I took off by ourselves on our adventures, but today Mom accompanied us. Perhaps with a purpose. I watched her as I spun. She was parked on a bench, smoke in hand, gabbing to an elderly couple. She seemed deep in conversation but she always had one eye on her kids.

Mom was bone thin; her top weight was 100 lbs. when she was pregnant. She laughed at her wedding picture and said that people said she and my dad had just left the TB sanitarium; they were both so skinny when they married. Her brown hair was always perfectly coiffed and she never went out of the house without dressing appropriately for the occasion. She was made up and wearing her engagement ring and wedding ring and some costume jewelry to accessorize her outfit. She wore a sleeveless seersucker dress with patch pockets with cherries on them. The full skirt and tight belt emphasized her tiny waist and petite frame. Her manicured nails on her beautiful hands matched her red lipstick.

Mom was small boned but she had an aggressive countenance. Maybe this was because of her significant overbite, the result of experimental braces in childhood. She had a wide smile and bright hazel eyes. Perpetually tan, with an aquiline nose, there was something just this side of regal in her bearing. She often held her head back and cocked slightly to the side which made her appear as if she was looking down her nose at you, even if you were two feet taller than her. Although her ancestry harkened back to pre-Revolutionary times and she was proud of her DAR membership, with her high cheekbones and olive skin, she made me think of a Native American warrior princess.

As we played, screams came from the apartment building across the street. We had heard those screams before. A woman, barefoot, dressed only in a slip and hair a mess, ran towards the playground. She had a young boy with glasses in tow. She entered the playground and begged the adults for help and a dime to call the police. Her Bluto like husband was not far behind. Wearing a filthy, ripped undershirt with holes in it, pants that hung below his fat gut, and shoeless, he screamed obscenities at the meek woman and child. He was bald and unshaven and his appearance shocked us. Our father was a meticulous dresser who changed his clothes several times a day. Dad had his thick black hair cut weekly; there was never a hair out of place. He had a heavy beard and so he shaved twice daily, no five o'clock shadow for him. He had beautiful blue eyes and everyone said he looked like Tyrone Power. He was meticulously groomed and I sometimes thought Dad was grooming away the dirt and smell of smoke, fires, and death. The contrast was so shocking; we had never seen anything like it.

"Don't give that bitch any money" the bruiser shouted. No one moved. Then Mom's eyes flashed, her fighting Irish rose, and she stood ten feet taller than her 5'4" height. She walked calmly to the sobbing woman, opened her purse, and said, "Here's a dime—call the cops." The brutish husband threatened our mom again. "Don't give her any money." Mom pretended not to hear the 250 lb., 6'4" beast, and cajoled, "Here's some more money, take it, take some more. Take as much as you need." Barb and I had drawn closer to Mom and watched with fear and admiration. The Babies whimpered a little, they later remembered that they thought the bad man might hit Mom. We reassured them that everything would be ok.

The bruiser's victim started to inch towards the playground exit to call the police, when her brute husband rand ahead to the gate, shut it and locked everyone in. He barricaded our escape with his fat stomach and fists. "You're not going anywhere" he bellowed. Helen strode right up to the metal gate and confronted Bluto. "Open this gate—now!" she ordered. The fat creep was taken aback, and then he swore again and punched the gate with his huge fists. Mom never flinched. "I know who you are—I know your record—Schaeffer." She spat the man's name at him like it was an epithet.

Mom lived by a set of complex rules, a combination of Catholicism and the mores and morals of the 20s, 30s, and 40s. This gave her an exaggerated sense of justice. I always thought she really believed those Frank Capra movies where the little guy won. She held her family to much higher standards than she held the rest of the world. She was well-known to be a soft touch for anyone with a sob story and we never knew how much money she had given to people in need.

Her devout Catholicism taught her kindness to strangers, but this was no stranger—this was a wife beater and a bully. "Open this gate, you yellow bellied drunk. How dare you treat your wife and child this way? Shame on you, you chicken." The brute looked a bit bewildered, and swore at my mother again. Then she hit him with, "I am going to tell my husband, Jack Solick about this, Schaeffer."

Suddenly, the evil giant turned white and his belligerence collapsed. My mother turned on her heels and marched back to comfort the crying woman and her little boy. The brute was on my mother's heels. At first we thought he might assault her, but when she turned around, he fell on his knees, pleading, "Don't tell Jack Solick, lady, please, it will mean my job. I'm sorry, I'm sorry." Mom fired back, "Don't you apologize to me, apologize to them." She pointed at his wife and son. Then she taunted him, "I am telling him, I am telling Jack."

"No," he begged.

"I am telling."

The episode ended when the cops, dispatched from the Garfield Park precinct, arrived on the scene. Mom chatted with them; she knew them both from high school dances. Mom was popular and a great jitter bugger. The cops escorted Schaeffer from the playground and they drove off in the squad car. The meek wife thanked Mom and Mom gave her more money to buy her son an ice cream from the Good Humor truck making its rounds of the local playgrounds.

I often wondered where she got her guts. She moved through the world with an air of righteousness. Sometimes, as a kid, her outspoken, opinionated manner embarrassed me, but I knew she would always defend me. Maybe she honed her nerve as a girl. My grandfather was an alcoholic and Mom complained that my grandmother had sent her to the bars on Madison Street to demand my grandfather's paycheck from him before he spent it all treating everyone in the gin mill.

And there was Jack Solick. My father was the safety net that allowed her to stifle any fear or humility. They had each other's backs. Mom would often tell someone off with, "I don't need to take this—I have a husband, Jack Solick." Just the mention of his name bolstered her position. My dad was a brave and stoic man, a man of his word who trusted and treasured his family. His strength, quiet endurance, and integrity were well-known and people also knew not to cross him.

When my dad saw Schaeffer at the firehouse the next day, he got right to the point. He confronted the hulk. "You won't have to worry about your job, Schaeffer," my dad said quietly. "If you ever bother my wife and kids again, I'll kill you." Schaeffer knew that my dad meant it. Between my mom and my dad, there would be no more trouble with Schaeffer. There were no abuse hotlines in those days, but there was HELEN.

Both of my parents were quick tempered and I remember arguments about everything that would start from the minute my dad walked in the door from the firehouse. But every morning, I would wake up to the smell of bacon, eggs, and coffee. I would sneak a peek into the kitchen. Mom would be ironing Dad's uniform, making breakfast, cigarette glowing in the ashtray on the pink Formica table. Dad would be reading the morning paper in silence. It was their nice quiet moment, just the two of them, before he left for the firehouse and the horrors he fought against every day. Dad would kiss Mom before he left. It was their private moment. They might have been through hell the night before, but they started each day with a smile and a kiss. It was Helen and Jack against the world.

Stars in Our Eyes

The Smile Club

"Lights. Camera."

"Alright, girls, look at the cameraman, that's right."

"Keep looking right into the camera and give us a beautiful smile!"

"Five, four, three, two, one—you're on."

1955 was an important year for me. I turned seven and I learning cursive writing, mastered multiplication tables, wrote my first novel, and starred on a television show.

At this time, television was still new technology. Flat screens and Blu-ray were a long way off. The local television station, WGN, pioneered children's programming and broadcasted many live shows throughout the day—*Ding Dong School*, *Garfield Goose*, *Kukla, Fran and Ollie*, *Two Ton Baker the Music Maker*, and the *Smile Club*. Preschool programs were a novelty then. Younger sister, Barb, and I thought it was a good thing these shows were on television. Mom did not like getting up early; she was a night owl. So we learned not to disturb her. Instead, in the mornings before I went off to kindergarten, we would park ourselves in front of the television with a bowl of Kellogg's Frosted Flakes. We would make our bowl of Frosted Flakes with an extra touch—we poured tons of sugar on top of the cereal, and then drank the sweet sugared milk at the bottom of the bowl!!! It was delicious.

We'd flip on the television and follow along with *Ding Dong School*'s Miss Frances, as if we were already in class. We tried to get Mom up for the parent briefing at the end of the show, but Mom was still snoozing, so we listened instead. When we started kindergarten, Mom enrolled us in the afternoon class so she could sleep in. We still followed the same shows and the same routine before we went to school. Parked in the living room in our nightgowns, we would play along with the TV hosts. I learned to print, and began entering drawings and contests, but my big break came in second grade when I began cursive writing. I'd fill out the entry blanks in my large, childish pen, carefully shaping the large and small letters, making sure not to lift my pencil. I thought my handwriting masked my age—and I would check the box indicating I had a parent's permission to enter the drawing. Maybe I even forged Mom's name. Or maybe I had asked her permission, I was always careful to make the request when she was on the telephone so I knew I would get a "Yes, now stop interrupting me."

I desperately wanted a pet. I brought home stray cats that I found in the alley. They did not make it past the back door, so I would give them to a friend. By this time our pet fish Cleo had met her untimely demise, and I continued to fantasize about keeping horses in our backyard. I figured the horse would know to move if a truck pulled into the loading dock to deliver groceries to the restaurant. My mom thought I was crazy. She said that a horse could not live in the back alley but I was not convinced.

I had seen how strong and resourceful Gene Autry's horse was, and I was sure my horse would be just as smart. I saw myself as an urban Annie Oakley, riding the cement range, with my sister in tow.

My hair in pigtails, cowgirl hat on my back, secured against the Chicago winds by a stampede chin strap—I fantasized about riding my horse by Chicago landmarks like the Art Institute, and the Sun Times building. We would right wrongs, save abandoned animals, and help kids in need. We would feed the horses sugar and apples. I even named our horses and knew what they would look like. My horse would be a palomino named Ginger, and Barb's horse would be all white and named Sugar. I had a plan to acquire this beautiful animal and my soon to be faithful friend. I saw an ad in a comic book for salve. I could sell boxes of the balm to relatives, friends, and neighbors. Everyone would buy the salve, of course, and I would get a horse for Barb and me

I had started reading the back pages of the *Chicago Tribune* before I went to school. I figured out the words in the captions below the pictures on the last page when Barb and I were photographed at North Avenue Beach. I was pouring water on her head and she was upset when the *Trib* photographer asked me to look his way and smile. Maybe I got the celebrity bug then. By the second grade I figured that "I had this reading thing down" and devoured anything in print. I liked reading the cereal boxes in the morning.

My golden business opportunity appeared in the back of a Superman comic book. I was perusing the latest issue when the ad in the back screamed, "Make Money Now. Win valuable prizes selling our salve to friends and family." The ad in the comic book boasted that the salve "cures everything from athletes' foot to zygomycosis." I did the math; I knew my times tables. At a quarter a tube I'd only need to sell 1200 tubes to get a horse. I knew I'd found a winner. I filled out the entry blank with care. I ordered the maximum number of cases allowed, and filling in my address and postal code. I borrowed a stamp and envelope from Mom and walked to the corner mailbox. I dropped it in the slot and waited for the salve to arrive.

And arrive my order did —crates and crates came to the house while I was at school one day. Mom did not blink when the deliveryman rang the doorbell. "Take it all back—she's seven." The deliveryman nodded, "I've got a kid, too." When I came home, Mom asked what I thought I was doing. I patiently explained my master plan to hitch up horses in the cement back yard and she laughed and repeated the words lethal to my business plan, "We live in an apartment, you can't keep a pet here. It's cruel."

My days as a child tycoon ended before they began. This temporary setback did not deter me from my course of action. I kept my hand in by clipping coupons from the cornflake box, and sending away for toys like plastic submarines. I filled the little subs with baking soda and sent them diving in our enormous bathtub on legs. Barb kept track of the drawings and contests announced on the kids' shows.

Then they announced a drawing on WGN TV. Some lucky girl or boy whose name would be selected would win a dog. Not just any dog—a cocker spaniel. A dog wasn't a horse or a cat, but a dog was enough for me. I knew Mom would never let me have a cat, but maybe I could get her to agree to the dog if I caught her while she was on the phone.

A large desk stood in the apartment foyer. Mom said it belonged to Daddy when he attended boarding school at Campion in Wisconsin. It was filled with writing supplies, postcards, stamps, pencils, and pens. Mom said no one would move it down the three flights of stairs and out of the apartment. There was a stove stuffed in the front closet so I believed her. I found a postcard and filled out my name and address. I said I wanted a dog. I wanted to give him a good home and would feed and walk him every day. I addressed it to the television station and walked to the corner to the mailbox that I kept busy with my entry blanks. I crossed my fingers and dropped it in the box.

I forgot about the contest for a while. Second grade was a busy time. I prepared for my first communion, wrote my first novel, practiced my multiplication tables, took tap dancing lessons—I had a full schedule. So I was actually surprised when I came home from school one day and Mom told me the good news: "The TV station called. You won a dog. When did you enter the contest?" Before I could answer, she dashed my dreams with, "I told them you could not keep a dog in an apartment." My face fell, but Mom had a consolation prize. "They still want you to be on the show—and you get out of school!"

I would be pulled out of school for a day. That was better than winning a dog. I would be a VIP. Only kids who pneumonia, measles, or something else communicable had got to stay home from school. I let out a yelp and did a tap dance. Barb clapped her hands. Of course, she would be appearing with me: we were the Solick Sisters.

Barb and I fantasized about what it would be like to appear on television. We were sure it would be glamorous and splendid. We would have our own dressing rooms and makeup artist. We had seen the Hollywood musicals where the unknown understudy goes on to save the show and becomes a big star. Secretly, I felt sure they would recognize what a natural performer I was, and ask me to be a regular on the show. After all, I hadn't I been entertaining my family for years, staging shows on top of the cedar chest for anyone who would watch? I would be discovered, at last.

Mom called the principal, Sister Veronica Ann, and explained we would miss school on the day of our appearance. Barb and I told all our school friends. They were excited and promised to watch our television debut. Mom called all our relatives as well and told them we would be on television.

Barb and I planned and plotted for the big day. We had it all figured out - what we would say, how we would dress, and how everyone would see what clever, beautiful and talented girls we were. Mom took us to Barnett's Children's Store on Cicero Avenue where she bought us matching outfits down to the socks, shoes, and petticoats for our television premier. We would wear little plaid skirts with white blouses with Peter Pan collars rimmed with lace. Coordinating cardigans and saddle shoes completed the ensemble. Then we waited and watched the show every day, prepping for the big moment, rehearsing what we might say. The night before the big day, Mom set our hair in pin curls and we slept with the bobby pins poking in our ears. What price, beauty.

Finally, and not too soon for impatient little girls, the big day arrived. Mom came to my second grade classroom and told Sister Florence Marie that we were leaving for the television show. All the kids in the classroom *oohed* with envy. Mom had Barb with her and Dad was waiting downstairs in the car, a '53 yellow Chevy BelAir with a black roof. Donna, the baby, stayed home with Grandma to watch the show. Dad was allowed to take an hour's vacation time off to drive us. It was a straight shot down Madison Street to the Prudential Building, the tallest building in Chicago! Visiting the tallest building in Chicago and going up in the elevator was a really big deal to us. The Prudential Building had opened in 1955. It was first skyscraper built in 21 years, and WGN's antenna topped the 41 story building.

Dad could not stay for the show. Instead, he drove right back to the firehouse after kissing us goodbye on Randolph Street. He promised he'd be watching the show, and told us we were his stars. When we entered the Prudential Building lobby, we went up, up, up in the elevator to the television studio. The elevator opened to a closed door that had a tiny window. Mom knocked and then a man peeked at us through the tiny window. He was wearing a first mate's cap. It was Two Ton Baker's sidekick, Boson Bob. Bob smiled and opened the door to our television debut. "Hello girls! You must be the stars of the *Smile Club*." We nodded. Mom ushered us in to the tiny dressing room, but not before we noticed that Two Ton Baker was sailing on a cardboard ship and that the studio was not on the ocean free.

I had expected bright lights and a makeup mirror in the dressing room, but the surroundings were a bit worn and had all the trappings of a busy studio—cups with half-drunken coffee and curdled cream, half-eaten ham sandwiches, cigarette butts in ashtrays, and girly calendars. At first, I felt a bit disillusioned, where was the magic? The tawdry surroundings seemed creepy to me, but soon I got into the swing of things. Mom put a little lipstick and rouge on us and combed our hair again. The actors on the set were really nice. They made a big fuss over us and acted as if we were the only girls who had ever been on the show. Barb and I thought they were very familiar looking. The dentist looked just like Boson Bob. Later, we realized many of the actors played multiple roles on the children's shows. We felt right at home, we were pros. From the wings we watched Two Ton Baker singing, banging on the old piano; he was one of our favorites. We waited for our cue.

Then we were escorted on to the set. Barb and I took our places in an oversized dentist's chair. Mom stood on the sidelines watching, smiling, and giving us the thumbs up. The "dentist" host took his place, as did the puppeteer. Five, four, three, two, one—we were on! The lights were so hot that we started to sweat. They seemed blinding. Our little legs stuck to the leatherette seat of the fake dental chair. The puppets, OK and DK, looked a lot like scrub brushes attached to mop handles with faces drawn on the back of the brushes. The dentist introduced us and began to ask us questions about our diet and dental hygiene. The show was supposed to be educational, after all. And we tried to answer each question truthfully—in fact, we were brutally honest.

It was no secret that our Mom did not like to cook. She bragged about being a rotten cook and how she hated cooking and housework. We responded candidly to every single question that the dentist and his puppet sidekicks asked us regarding eating healthy foods candidly. The irony of being on a show about dental hygiene was not lost on us. We ate candy by the fistfuls; M & Ms were a mainstay of our diet. The dentist began his interrogation:

"Does your mother cook you lots of carrots?

"NO, but our grandmother does!"

"Do you eat your broccoli?"

"When my grandmother cooks it."

"How about your potatoes?"

"When my grandmother comes over on Sunday and cooks dinner for us."

In an attempt to help our host out, I asked, "Does Coke have vegetables?

"No!"

OK shook his head in dismay and DK snickered.

The dentist asked us about every vegetable and fruit, or anything food related and healthy in hopes that we would say that "Mom cooked something." We consistently replied,

"No, but our grandmother cooks that for us!"

The litany of fruits and vegetables ended, and they cut to a commercial. The crew was grinning and told us we were doing great. Then we were on again.

Back at the firehouse on Fulton and Kilpatrick, the whole company was tuned in to *The Smile Club*. These men, who braved death and tragedy every day, exploded with hysterical laughter at our conversation with the dentist. Daddy said the firemen agreed it was the funniest thing they had ever seen. Mom went on and on about our interview, saying that all her friends had called her and accused her of not feeding her kids. She ate up all the attention and was not at all insulted—Mom loved the spotlight!

Barb and I had our thirty minutes of fame and then, as quickly as it had begun, the show was over. The dentist and puppets thanked us for being on the show and gave us lots of goodies, like a Two Ton Baker record album, to take home.

The next day when we went back to St. Mel's School, the shout rang out: "There they are!" I felt like we were at Hollywood movie premiere. Basking in the applause, we were surrounded by our classmates. They pressed close to hear every detail. A boy stepped on my saddle shoes as he leaned forward. One girl offered us her Jujubes. Everyone wanted to be our friend. The kids bombarded us with questions.

"We watched the show. You guys were great."

"Is Two Ton Baker really that fat or does he wear pillows?"

"Is the boat real?"

"How do they make the puppets talk?"

"Did you get to keep all the prizes?

"Can I have your autograph?"

"Did they pay you?"

We regaled the kids with our experiences like old veterans. Basking in the glory of our television debut, we even signed autographs. We never did get the dog or the horses—but Barb and I agreed that being on television was better than having a pet, anyway.

We were stars!

The Banjo's Back in Town

The only mementos I have of the Variety Shows are some out-of-focus black and white snapshots taken with a Brownie Camera, a crumbled program printed on mimeograph paper that we found in my mother's attic after she died, and a home movie of a school chorus with no sound that was posted on the alumni Facebook page. Those shabby souvenirs remind me of a time when I was a kid and the annual St. Mel–Holy Ghost School Variety Show was a rite of passage every spring.

The musical extravaganza was THE event of the year. For months in advance after-school activities were focused on the fundraiser, and keeping little 'thugs' off the street. Father Shaughnessy, the priest who headed all the youth programs at our parish, was the self-appointed director and promoter. He gave the show a big build-up and everyone in the school wanted to be involved. Best of all, every child was guaranteed a spot in the show if they wanted it—but the big deal was to land a solo act.

The proceeds from the week-long performances were always donated to charity. I remember a kid who lost his leg jumping freight trains on the railroad tracks that bisected our neighborhood being the stimulus for one of the first shows. There was a worthy cause every year, and we inner city kids were encouraged to volunteer and raise money for the less fortunate. We did not realize we were the 'slum kids'. The event was so successful that it became a much anticipated annual program for the whole community. For months before the June performances, Father Shaughnessy would hold auditions and rehearsals in the grammar school basement. The show was held for five nights after school let out for the summer and ticket sales benefited some new charity or unfortunate case. Local merchants signed on to promote the show with signs in their windows. They donated prizes to give to the kids who sold the most tickets—$1 a pop—and Donna Tristano always won the top prize which was a bike or some other coveted item.

Early in the school year, Barb and I set our sights on a solo number. We'd never been in the Variety Show before and figured, "Why not start at the top?" We had a plan and thought we had a great number—"Honey Bun". We had taken dance lessons at Mayblossom McDonald's after all and the fact that my voice was like Alfalfa's was no impediment since I would lip sync the song. I was a seasoned performer—I'd been dancing and singing on top of the cedar chest for a select audience since I was two years old.

Barb and I both loved movies and we had become obsessed with South Pacific when it was released in 1958. We saw the film, featuring Mitzi Gaynor, Rossano Brazzi, and Ray Walston in glorious Technicolor at our favorite Marbro Theater and were enchanted. We saved our pop bottle return money and bought a used copy of the movie soundtrack from Garrett's Music City down the block on Madison Street. We learned all the words to the musical numbers and practiced every day after school, playing the album over and over again on the record player that Uncle Billy left us after he moved out of our apartment. Barb and I decided I would dress up in my Dad's old Navy uniform, he was not a tall man, but I would still be swimming in it. I would play the Nellie Forbush part and Barb, who was tiny, would wear a hula skirt and play the Luther Billis role.

We were sure we would be the hit of the show. Who could fail to see the humor of a ten-year-old and her much shorter eight-year-old sister singing a Broadway showtune?

Barb and I must have played that album thousands of times, singing along, "A hundred and one pounds of fun..." over and over and over again, mugging and prancing before our imaginary audience. Finally, after the Christmas holidays, the auditions were announced by Sister Veronica Ann over the school public address system. Barb and I got to the auditions early so we could grab a seat in the front row. The folding chairs were set up on the assembly hall linoleum floor. Hundreds of kids from the entire neighborhood packed the grammar school basement. St. Mel's students in their uniforms and Tilton School kids in after-school play clothes all came to try out because this was an egalitarian affair and every kid in the neighborhood was welcome. The smells of Double Bubble bubble gum, peanut butter, graham crackers, butch wax and overripe bananas filled the warm basement with a heady juvenile perfume.

Father Shaughnessy raised a hand and everyone was silent. "OK—let me hear from Mary McCarty," and Mary belted out, "If You're Irish Come into the Parlor" sure to be a hit with many in the neighborhood. "You're in," Father Shaughnessy pronounced the words of success.

Barb sat still but I squirmed and fidgeted and bit my nails while the parade of Irish dancers, roller skaters, baton twirlers, child tenors, musicians, and acrobats rolled by. The auditions seemed to go on forever. Finally, as Barb began to nod off, we heard, "Solick Sisters—you're up." We ran to the front of the hall and nodded to

Sister Charlotte Marie who cued up our album to the right track. We nailed it like old vaudevillians. We tapped our best feet forward, in my case already a size 8. As I glided across the floor, I tried to gauge the audience response. They seemed to love it.

When the song ended, Father Shaughnessy declared, "Congratulations, Solicks—you're in." We ran home to tell our Mom the great news. She told us that she knew we would make the cut. Everyone would make the cut, we sniffed, we were after something bigger. For months after the auditions, we would rehearse our acts in that school basement, practicing for the big day— "Another opening, another show" was the first number of the Variety Show, and everyone who wanted to perform could sing in the chorus. We practiced at home, in the backyard, in the schoolyard, in front of anyone who would watch us. Barb, who was the dancer and artist in the family, drilled me on my steps and my Mom coached me on my dramatic gestures. We would strut our stuff for any audience, adults, classmates, Aidan Lennon and his dog— anyone. And every day, we ran to the grammar school basement to rehearse our number for Father Shaughnessy. We were sure we were just getting better and better.

So we were stunned one day after we had performed our number, and Father Shaughnessy invited Sheila Kissane and Linda Hunt up to the front of the hall. We had seen them watching us perform and huddling with Father Shaughnessy, but had not given it any thought; he said we were in the show. And, I was flabbergasted as they cued up my record album that I had saved to purchase, and the two girl athletes performed our number. The outrage dawned on me—they were trying to steal our act and did not even have the decency to go buy their own used album. Barbara was almost in tears by the end of the song and I was furious but confident. Anyone could see these lumbering jocks had nothing on the Solick Sisters. Their performance was wooden and clumsy and I thought they looked like they were playing basketball. My friends, my sister and I agreed that they'd have to bring out the bomb sniffing dogs if these two appeared on stage. But Father Shaughnessy, who also was an athlete, thought otherwise. Sheila and Linda were two of his "pets" and he announced there would be an elimination and he would be the judge of who would perform the number.

I was almost shaking and ran all the way home from school down Madison Street and up three flights of stairs, pulling Barb along with me, to tell my mother about fickle Father Shaughnessy. Choking back tears of rage, I told my mother about the injustice, but she seemed nonplussed.

"You know he favors those athletes. Those girls' legs look like tree trunks." Her critique was small comfort to us. If there was one thing our parents had taught us it was that life was not fair.

We had a pretty good idea what the outcome would be. And even though Father Shaughnessy dragged out the agony of the elimination round with two teams rehearsing for weeks, in the end, he announced what we knew was coming—Kissane and Hunt would perform the number. All our work and creativity was down the drain.

"Well, you'll just have to come up with a better act. I wasn't that crazy about that song anyway."

Mom was a pragmatist. She taught us to "pick yourself up, dust yourself off, and start all over again." It was back to the drawing board. I racked my ten-year-old brain. What could I do now with so little time left? It seemed like a plot from an old Gene Kelly movie. Then I came up with an idea and Barb chimed in.

"What about a Roaring Twenties song?"

Barb added, "You could do the Charleston and all your friends could be part of the act."

The little ballerina and acrobat, Barb would work out the dance numbers. We could practice the chorus line in the cement backyard now that the weather was nice. But we had to find the song. We took off running down Madison Street past the fortune teller's parlor to Garrett's and began shuffling furiously through the stacks of used record albums. One dusty album caught my eye, Little Miss Hitmaker, Teresa Brewer, and the song, "The Banjo's Back in Town." I remembered the tune had been a hit on the radio a few years before. It had a chorus and a 1920s theme. I thought it was perfect. We went into the sound booth to listen to the track. With our headphones on, Barb and I nodded to each other. This was the one. I plunked my quarter down on the counter. Barb and I ran home with our prize. Mom even relinquished the telephone and we called the girl chorus members to come and practice at our house the next day.

My grade school chums did not have solo numbers in the Variety Show and they were excited to be a part of the new act. They also wanted revenge because they, too, thought the judging was unfair and that Barb and I should not have been edged out of the show. We all vowed this would be the best act ever and we would show everyone. I would be the front person, mimicking Teresa Brewer. Barb would teach all the girls the Charleston and drilled them on the dance. Mom, still dreaming of a career with the Rockettes, provided suggestions and an artistic critique of our act. We practiced all week and then we were ready for tryouts.

We didn't bother to change, but headed to the assembly hall still dressed in our school uniforms, blue serge jumpers that we wore sometimes for weeks on end without washing. The uniforms were indestructible. Made of some compound like the material in The

Man in the White Suit, no amount of puddles, playgrounds, dirt lots, football games, jump rope, or fights could damage this fabric. No matter how hard we tried to tear or rip the uniforms, they survived to be passed on to the next child in line; the wear tracks from alterations were the only clue that these grade school fatigues had been worn before. I knew we would have to really sell this song to be transformed from parochial school inmates in hand me down uniforms to jazz age cuties. We waited through the rehearsals for the right moment to approach the now hated Father Shaughnessy. When the rehearsals seemed to lag, I marched to the front of the hall with the album in hand and confronted him—"We have a new act to try out."

He seemed to hesitate as he was taken off guard by me, the pint-sized impresario, and I gestured to our troupe to get up here quickly. I handed the album to Sister Charlotte Marie and pointed out the track I wanted to play.

And as the ragtime number pealed out in the basement of St. Mel's School, I mugged and hammed it up and danced my heart out. I had to do this, not just for me, but for my sister and all the girls who were backing me up. I kicked my heels and whirled and twirled imaginary beads. Before I knew it, the song was over and the hall erupted in applause.

We looked over at Father Shaughnessy, the Ziegfeld of St. Mel-Holy Ghost Church was grinning. "You're in!"

We did it, we pulled it off. We'd landed a spot in the Variety Show! All our friends gathered around to congratulate us.

The next few weeks were a blur of rehearsing and planning and designing our costumes. My mother, who had a great flair for the dramatic, was self-appointed wardrobe mistress and makeup artist.

She enlisted her Italian American Aunt Camille, a great seamstress, to make our flapper costumes.

Aunt Camille, always good for costumes on short notice, came up with a fabulous design. I requested a green satin chemise with rows of black fringe and Barb asked for her signature color, blue. We wore sequined headbands with feathers. We were amazed that other people stepped up and offered to help with props. The nuns at the school made banjos for the chorus line to strum complete with glitter and neon paint. Since all the girls could not afford to have costumes made, my mother rummaged for jewelry, feather boas and scarves. She would make sure that every girl felt like a star that opening night.

During the weeks prior to the first performance, I sensed that all was not well with the "Honey Bun" crew. Their performance never got any better. And the girls became openly hostile to me at school, kicking me from the pew behind when we went to Mass every day. I didn't get it. They got what they wanted, so I couldn't figure out why they were mad.

As the oldest child in the family, I did not have a concept of what jealousy was. I always had what I wanted or I would try to get it myself or I knew my parents couldn't afford it, so forget it. I saw myself as a protector of the younger and weaker kids and was always ready to take on the local bullies. But I could not understand what these girls were upset about. I was too busy with the rehearsals anyway and decided to ignore them as long as they did not bug my little sister. Eventually, Father Shaughnessy decided to ramp up the humor and replaced Linda with one of the football players dressed in drag and wearing a mop head for a wig. I still didn't think it was funny.

Finally, the big night arrived. The shows were staged in the St. Mel Boy's High School gym and auditorium, with a real stage and lights. The house was packed. My grandparents, aunts, uncles and cousins were all seated in the audience. My mother was backstage in the locker room putting the finishing touches on all the girls' makeup. We heard the applause and the opening chorus belting out, "There's No Business like Show Business." I started to get nervous and sweaty and bit my nails some more. What if this was a bomb? What if we were duds? What if we stank? What if, what if? I took a deep breath, I knew I could not let my sister or the gang down and I could not lose my nerve. They were all depending on me to pull it off.

Then I heard Father Shaughnessy command, "Solick, you're up next."

We waited in the wings for our cue watching the Irish Tenor boy sing, "Come back to Erin, Mavourneen, Mavourneen..." Then everything went dark. The glittered and fluorescent painted banjoes glowed iridescent in the black lights. Father Shaughnessy had arranged for the special effects. I caught my breath and when the music played, Charlestonned out on the stage, twirling the long string of beads around my neck.

I don't know if the audience was unprepared for a troupe of eight and ten-year-old girls dressed up in false eyelashes and flapper dresses, but a roar came from the audience. When the lights came back up they were so bright, I could not see well, but I thought I spied my Dad, Gram and Gramps, Aunt Camille and her family beaming and clapping their hands. It seemed like the two minutes and thirty seconds went by so fast as I danced with my girls in front of a packed house. The song ended. The seconds before the audience reacted seemed like a century.

And then, the audience was on their feet cheering and applauding for more. They demanded an encore and we performed the song again. No crowd had ever asked for an encore. We were the hit of the show. The banjo was back in town.

The next four nights were just as successful. The audiences yelled for more and we gave it to them. Barb and I, and later my youngest sister Donna, became the Solick Sisters and headliners of the Variety Show every year as long as we attended St. Mel-Holy Ghost School.

But that night, my parents took the troupe to Elite's to celebrate our triumph and treated all the girls to hot fudge sundaes, chocolate malts and French fries. We rested on our laurels and looked forward to a summer of swimming pools, sleeping late, and playing all day with our friends. There would be no homework, no mean girls, no contests, and school could wait until the fall.

The Major and the Minor

Like most girls in the neighborhood, and like our mother before us, we began our dance lessons at Mayblossom MacDonald's Ideal Dance Studio. The dance studio was on an upper floor of a commercial building at the same location where my mother studied dance. Every Saturday, starting when we were five and three years old, Barbara and I would pack up our ballet slippers and practice outfits, and Mom would walk us down Madison Street towards Garfield Park. We'd stop just short of the Park and climb the narrow staircase to Ideal Dance Studio. When we came to the third floor, we'd stop at the receptionist's desk. Lovely sepia tone professional photographs of the owner, Mayblossom MacDonald, dressed in glittery costumes taken in her heyday, covered the walls behind the desk. A striking ballerina, who also taught lessons part-time at the studio, greeted us by name, and Mom fished in her purse and pulled out $2 —a dollar a piece for our lessons. Then Mom would waltz us back to the changing room where we would slip on our ballet slippers and togs. The atmosphere was serene. The polished wood floors, the large rooms with high ceilings, the floor to ceiling mirrors on every practice room wall, and the ballet barres where we practiced our positions—the school was like a sanctuary.

We took our positions at the barre and waited for Miss MacDonald to make her entrance. The grande dame had been a star in the 1920s. Silver-haired and still beautiful, she continued to manage the school and oversaw the dance lessons with the help of her lovely, much younger assistants. Dressed in a wide legged, cotton jumpsuit, Miss MacDonald called the room to attention.

"Attention, s'il vous plait, young ladies. Assume the first position." Miss MacDonald nodded to her assistant, and the young woman cued up the classical music. The assistant would take us through the exercises that day and every day. We knew the venerable Miss MacDonald was older than our Gram. She'd taught our mother to dance. Still, we admired and respected her energy; Mom told us she'd been a great dancer in her day.

"First position, second position, third position, fourth position, fifth position. Ladies, remember your arms."

The assistant would pace the room while we practiced, coaching, correcting, and demonstrating the dance moves. She was so lovely and kind that sometimes I would position my feet incorrectly just so she would take time to coach me personally. The Ideal dance instructors treated each girl with dignity and respect whatever their ability. Miss MacDonald would often paraphrase Isadora Duncan.

"Young ladies, you are born to dance. We dance in the womb."

Barbara needed no coaching; she was the artist and the dancer in the family. When the dance instructor demonstrated a series of steps for our recital, Barbara knew them on her first attempt. I practiced and practiced, but never achieved Barbara's natural grace. Not that it mattered too much to me, I just wanted to dress up in costumes and clown around at the dance studio and on the stage. Like the ballerina on my jewelry box, Barbara pirouetted to the music— tiny, lithe, and perfect.

Miss MacDonald still had connections and my mother was thrilled to learn our dance recital would be at Chicago's Civic Opera House. Weekly we'd climb the stairs to the studio to drill on our routine. The youngest girls' ballet class would perform a can-can to Maurice Chevalier's, "Oui, Oui Marie." Moms were given the patterns and a referral to dressmakers if unable to sew the costumes. There was no question for us, Mom wouldn't sew any costumes, but she had her support network. Mom's Aunt Camille was a great seamstress and she always came through for us with her sewing skills. The instructor showed us the illustration on the cover of the Vogue pattern package. Pink tea-length satin dresses with rows of silver ruffles stitched on the underside of the garment, trimmed with silver border and bow at the neckline. We were overjoyed— the dresses with matching tiny berets were charming. I pictured myself turning cartwheel after cartwheel across the stage.

Arriving at the Civic Opera House, I had one of the first of many childhood disillusionments. A fan of Hollywood movies, I imagined posh dressing rooms filled with flowers from adoring fans. But the reality was about as far from classy as you could get. The dressing rooms were more like grimy caves and years of dirt and grease paint were the only décor. Mom warned us not to touch anything. She had anticipated this and had done our hair and makeup at home, so all we had to do was slip on our can-can outfits and we were ready to dance. Well prepared, the recital went off without a hitch. Like a character from a Toulouse Lautrec playbill, I executed perfect splits at the end of my cartwheel and brought down the house.

But our days with Mayblossom's dance troupe were numbered. Mom was pregnant and after a few months, the trek down Madison Street was too taxing for her. We became young dropouts. Our costumes hung in the back closet looking forlorn until Mom shipped them off to our cousins in Washington. School activities and friends from Monroe Street filled our calendar.

Time passed. Barbara missed the dance lessons, but then we got busy with Variety Show practice and our triumph at the Civic Opera House became a memory. Then one day flyers were circulated around St. Mel's School announcing the opening of a new dance studio—Marjorie Minor's Academy of Dance. The circular promised affordable introductory lessons in ballet, tap, acrobatics, Irish dance, and exotic dance, whatever that was. Barb and I ran home after school with the flyers to badger Mom.

"Mom, Mom! There's a new dance studio. We want to take tap and ballet and acrobatics. And it is in the next block. We can walk ourselves."

"You quit ballet before. I'm not spending the money for shoes and costumes again."

"We didn't quit. You wouldn't take us anymore."

"No, you lost interest. I don't want that racket with the tap shoes in the house."

Barbara looked crestfallen, but I wouldn't admit defeat that easily. I waited until Mom was on the phone and then resumed my pitch.

"Mom, you took tap lessons when you were little and look what a good dancer you are. Please, come on," I entreated.

"What? I told you not to bother me when I am on the phone."

"Mom, you are on the phone all the time. Can I?"

"What? Yes. Stop interrupting me."

Barbara's eyes lit up. Success! If Mom balked, I would remind her she told us yes when she was talking on the telephone and hold her to her word.

Later that week, we ambled down to Red Goose shoes. The manager, a middle aged balding man who smelled like pipe tobacco and dressed in a jacket with patched elbows, spotted us right away as the girls he'd chased off his roof on many occasions. His eyes saucered in disbelief when the female hooligans who threw water balloons on his customers told him they needed dance shoes.

He addressed Barbara, "You, I believe it," and then he turned to me, "But you?"

"Tap shoes, please."

"Oh, of course. Then you can make a commotion all over your parents' house."

"Size eight, please."

"You got big feet, miss."

"Keeps me stuck to the ground."

This banter went on while we tried on shoe after shoe until we found the right fit. Barbara got ballet and tap shoes but I only wanted the tap shoes with the largest cleats I could find. Mom warned me to get my shoes a size bigger because my feet were growing so fast, faster than the rest of me. My dad, having been in the Navy, affectionately called my feet "gunboats." When Barbara and I had made our selections, we followed the manager to the counter to pay. Feeling very grown up, I peeled off the bills while he rang the total on the cash register and I paid for our shoes. The manager hefted the boxes over the counter and I carried them, tied with string, back to our apartment. We tore off the string, threw the box lids aside, ripped off the tissue paper, and donned our shoes. I immediately struck a pose and launched into my best Ethel Merman imitation. Warbling "I got rhythm, I got music..." at the top of my lungs until Mom yelled.

"Shaddup! You sound like a banshee. I just got those babies to sleep. I thought you were taking dance lessons, not singing lessons. If I'd known you were going to be a songstress, I could have saved the money you spent on those shoes."

"Mom, I thought I'd demonstrate my tap shoes for Aunt Marie." I deviously played to my mother's intense dislike of my father's aunt who lived in the apartment below us. Mom's eyes flashed a devilish glint and a sly grin spread over her face; she'd been a scamp when she was a kid and she never lost her love of a little mischief.

"All right, you can tap dance but cut that screeching out now."

Aunt Marie pounded with what sounded like a broom on the ceiling, but I kept on. When she pounded, I tried to tap a response back in the same number of beats. Like Rhoda in the Bad Seed, I continued with my best Ann Miller imitation for the next 45 minutes or so, until I got bored with harassing Aunt Marie and Barbara suggested we head over to the Lennon's house.

Saturday morning Barbara was awake early. Having slept poorly the night before, she said she felt sick. She always got sick when something exciting was going to happen.

"Don't worry. Just eat a small bowl of Frosted Flakes. It will make you feel better."

She moaned at my suggestion, but dutifully went to the pantry and retrieved the big box with Tony the Tiger on the cover and made herself a small bowl.

"Just a few bites. It will settle your stomach."

Then we skipped Mighty Mouse and our other favorite Saturday cartoons and started digging through the back closet to find our old dance cases. I hoped Mom hadn't sent them off to Washington with our costumes. I, at least, had grown too tall for the practice costumes. Barbara would be petite for her entire life and could wear her plaid grade school skirts when she was a married woman with her own children. But we could still use the cases to carry our new shoes. As luck would have it, Mom hadn't packed them up in one of her care packages. I tugged them out from under boxes of unsorted family photographs, dusted them off, and handed Barbara her blue case.

"They're still good. Let's use them."

We'd purchased black leotards and tights in the girls' department at Madigan's Store. Madigan's had everything! I ripped the cellophane and cardboard packaging off and stretched the tights over my skinny long legs. Tugging the leotard over the tights, I stood up, slipped on my tap shoes, and surveyed myself in the closet mirror. I thought I belonged on the Great White Way.

We tiptoed into Mom and Dad's bedroom. Mom was still snoozing, her head wrapped in toilet paper to preserve her coiffure. Dad had been at work for hours. I whispered.

"Mom, we're leaving. We're going to dance class now."

"Oh geez, what time is it? Are the babies still asleep? "

She opened her eyes a bit and barked.

"You're not walking down the street in those leotards. Get some clothes on."

"Mom, no, we don't have time to change. We gotta go. We'll be late."

"OK. Well, put your coats on and button them all the way."

"Let's go!" I dragged Barbara and grabbed our coats from the front closet and ran down the stairs to the street. We ran east on Madison to the studio. Up the stairs we vaulted, two at a time, my tap shoes clicking all the way.

Girls jammed a small entry way into the "studio"— just a rented room with a hardwood floor really. No one greeted us and there was no dressing room or lockers, so we set our coats and cases against the wall. A tall dark-haired woman with a clipboard checked the girls in. A younger version of the woman, just a few years older than me, stood next to her.

"I am Mrs. Minor, the director of the dance studio. I have danced professionally on the stage and appeared in many productions. I have also instructed professionals that have appeared on and off Broadway and television. Sharon is my daughter and she will assist me."

I immediately wondered what she was doing teaching us. Waiting my turn in the queue, I checked out the shabby décor. The studio lighting was dim and the walls dingy. There was only one ballet barre and a small mirror in the corner. I wondered how we would check ourselves out if there were no mirrors. No lovely ballet assistant would be taking us through the routines.

"What is your name? How old are you? When is your birthday? What dance lessons are you taking? Do you have your money?

When Mrs. Minor finished collecting her fees, she announced that she would be organizing everyone into classes and we were to stand with the group when our names were called. Barbara and I waited patiently.

"Anita and Barbara Solick. Mini Rockets"

I looked at Barbara. The Mini Rockets were all younger than me and much shorter. I wasn't a mini. I knew there must be a mistake. I approached Mrs. Minor.

"Excuse me, I am in 6th grade and you put me with my sister."

"That's right. You were born in October, right. Get back to your group if you want to dance here."

"Not that again—why don't these people understand I am nearly two years old than these kids?" I skulked back to the group after signaling to my friends that I wouldn't be able to join them. Barbara patted me in consolation.

"At least we're together."

Mrs. Minor walked to each group and demonstrated a few steps and then dismissed us all until the following Saturday. I wondered what we had paid for and I calculated how many candy bars I could have purchased with the $1 I'd handed off to Mrs. Minor as I tapped to twenty down Madison Street.

The next week Barbara was still enthused, so we headed back to the dance studio for another lesson. I would hang around after the class while Barbara took ballet so I could walk her home.

I couldn't wait to start making some noise with my taps, but the lesson proved a rude awakening for me. Apparently Mrs. Minor didn't think I was a budding Ruby Keeler. While I had envisioned myself tripping the light fantastic with Fred Astaire, Mrs. Minor didn't hold the same high opinion of my skills. In fact, she seemed to be bent on humiliating me, and would hold me up to ridicule before the younger girls. She went to great lengths to praise Barbara; she clearly didn't understand that we didn't compete against each other—we were sisters and stuck together.

"Anita, you are pigeon-toed. Anita, you are off the beat. Watch the younger girls. Have you practiced these steps at all? Shuffle, ball, change. Why don't you know these steps? Barbara, show her how to do it. Excellent, you've got it."

Even at my tender age, I disliked her calling me by my first name and I thought she was picking on me. This scene was repeated, week after week. I decided I liked the tap shoes, but not the dance instructor. But I couldn't disappoint Barbara so I continue to attend, enduring the public ridicule. After all, Barbara was always a willing sidekick when I had a scheme so I figured I owed her.

One week, though, I'd had enough. When Mrs. Minor began reciting the same litany of my tap dancing transgressions, I interrupted. "I thought I was paying for tap dancing lessons. Why aren't you teaching me? I'm not getting any better. Why don't you help me?"

Mrs. Minor looked shocked for just a moment and then came the retort in shrill voice tinged with sarcasm.

"Well, when you have no natural ability... I can't make a silk purse out of a sow's ear."

My face flushed; I leaned over to Barbara and spoke out of the side of my mouth

"That's it. I am quitting."

Later, Mrs. Minor brought in catalogs of dance costumes and order blanks. She proclaimed that we would have a recital soon and we needed to order our professional costumes. I grabbed one of the catalogs and flipped through the pages. "Yahoo," I rejoiced inside. I had my out. Mom would never pay this much money for the costumes. And she certainly wouldn't let us wear anything skimpy like this up on a stage. She'd have a fit. Mrs. Minor had marked the costume numbers that we should order. She'd selected a red, white and blue satin high cut jumpsuit with a halter top and sequins down the front. The revealing design made me cringe and I longed for my old can-can costume. I couldn't wait until Mom got a load of this. Then Mrs. Minor dropped the bombshell.

"And next week, dancers, prices are increasing. Please bring $3 per dance lesson."

I knew there was no way Mom would go for this. Barbara, who was the best dancer in the class, dragged her feet as we headed home. I didn't like to see her sad and tried to cheer her.

"Hey, Variety Show practice is starting soon and I have some great ideas for numbers. I need you to choreograph all of them for me and you will have a solo. Barb, come on, you know are a better dancer than everybody at that place—old bag teachers included." This seemed to console her. "Listen, this is my idea. How about a sisters' act and we can bring Donna in, too."

The sounds of American music from my parents' 78s, purchased when they were jitterbugging teens filled our home when I was a kid. I got my music education from the thick waxy records and from MGM musicals. I sang along and, by the time I was ten, I'd learned thousands of songs. Mom and Dad hit the nightclubs in Chicago almost every weekend to take in the headliners at the Chez Paree or one of the Chicago hot spots of the day. Gram would babysit and let us stay up after she went to bed to watch old horror movies on Shock Theater. The next day Mom would regale us with stories about Frank and Sammy and Mel. She told us that Mel Torme sang at their high school dances when she was young. I learned to love all the big bands, Count Basie, Duke Ellington, the Dorsey Brothers, and the great singers —Billie, Ella, and Joe Williams. The Andrews Sisters' kitschy tunes inspired me and I hatched a genius plan for the Solick Sisters.

"Barb, listen I really need your help. Here's what I've got in mind. We can sing *Boogie Woogie Bugle Boy*. No one has ever done a sisters' act. And the parents will love the song. It's a sure hit."

"We've can wear those army outfits that Uncle Billy got us. We'll have to get one for Donna. And you know what? We can go to two movie theaters on Saturday now if we aren't going to dance lessons."

And while I hummed the tune, Barbara began working on our dance steps. We hummed and danced our way home.

Still I didn't want to let Barbara down if she wanted to continue. We rang the buzzer and Mom yelled through the intercom, "Who's there?"

We yelled back, "It's us!" and she buzzed us in. Zipping up the stairs, I hit the third floor landing with a thud. Mom swung the heavy oak front door wide open.

"You sound like a herd of cattle."

"Mom, Mrs. Minor wants us to buy these outfits from this costume house. Our costumes are on page four. And she said the dance lessons are three bucks from now on." I handed the catalog off to Mom.

Her right eyebrow arched and her eyes narrowed in skepticism.

"She's getting a kickback. "

Then Mom laid eyes on the scanty jumpsuits. "She's nuts. I'm not going to let you wear these things. What does she think this is? A burlesque house? You are kids—not Gypsy Rose Lee, for God's sake"

Mom continued with her rant. "And 3 bucks for her to prance around like a Shetland pony while you two watch. Affordable introductory lessons, humph! Bait and switch. It's a swindle. The nerve of that broad."

I tried to repress my glee. We would not be going back to Marjorie Minor's Academy of Dance.

The next few months were crammed with activity and we forgot all about the dance lessons. Barbara, Donna and I rehearsed our sisters' act daily after school. Plugging in the old record player that Uncle Billy left us, we'd listen to the 78's again and again until we got the lyrics down. Fans of the TV show, *The Roaring Twenties,* Barb and I decided it would be really fun to dress little Donna up as a flapper and have her lip sync a Betty Boop song. Barbara took

Donna through the dance moves, and soon she was belting out the song like an old pro. And, much to my surprise, my old nemesis, Father Shaughnessy, tapped me to be Eloise, the heroine of the children's stories. I had to admit I was flattered, but my act had been the sensation of the show the previous year.

Father Shaughnessy liked to feature Broadway show tunes and popular hit songs in his shows every year. Kay Thompson had written the books and a dramatization for *Playhouse 90.* Thompson recorded the theme song, a minor hit in the 1950s. Father Shaughnessy let me pick my Nanny, so I persuaded Mary Lennon to play the role. If we all weren't practicing at our house, we would drag the old record player across the alley to the Lennon's and set it up on the back porch. Mrs. Lennon never minded. Then we'd run through all our routines under the clothesline in the cement backyard until it got dark and Mom yelled for us to get back home.

Then, a few weeks before opening day, a familiar face appeared at our rehearsals in the school basement.

"What's she doing here?" Barbara and I exchanged crusty looks but said nothing to anyone else.

Mrs. Minor stood in the front of the school basement assembly room conferring with Father Shaughnessy.

Then the priest announced, "This is Mrs. Minor. She has graciously volunteered to help choreograph the group numbers in the show. And she's agreed to perform herself."

Barbara and I shot a look at each other. I bit my cheeks so I wouldn't laugh out loud. Mrs. Minor bowed and gave a speech about turning this into a "professional" show.

Father Shaughnessy signaled rehearsals would begin and bellowed, "Eloise. Where's my Eloise? You're up first" and I ran up to the front, pulling Mary along to present our song.

On the way home, we giggled about a grown woman appearing in a children's show and patted ourselves on the back for creating our own acts and passing on the group numbers.

"Really, Barb, I never said anything, but I can't stand her. She is mean. I am glad we aren't in the chorus. Why does an old woman want to be in our kids' show?" Barbara and I had no answer for this. We just thought she was weird.

Patti Mullane tugged at my sleeve. She was out of breath, her eyes wide with shock.

"You better come fast. Mrs. Minor has gone nuts. She's throwing all your costumes out of the locker and dumping them on the floor!"

Barbara and I did a double take and raced down the linoleum tile floor to the converted boy's locker room that served as a dressing room for the Variety Show. The hand-lettered sign by the door read "Girls ONLY."

I ran so fast that when I got to the door I slid right through on the heels of my patent leather dress shoes. Mrs. Minor, our former dance teacher, was whirling like a dervish, flinging costumes and shoes in the air. Our pink and blue dance cases were upended and all the contents were strewn on the benches and the floor. Tall and slim, dressed in a revealing, high-cut black leotard and fishnet hose, her black hair disheveled, her menacing appearance instantly made me think of Medusa.

Mrs. Minor turned and shrieked something I couldn't understand and then charged at me. I instinctively pushed Barbara behind me.

"I am the star of the show. This room is mine. Get out, you brats. You think you are special. I am a professional."

I suppressed a laugh, thinking the woman was unhinged. I wanted to meet her ferocity with a serious demeanor. Although her anger frightened me a bit, I wouldn't back down. Barbara still hid behind me. I signaled her with a pat and whispered.

"Get Mom, NOW."

Mom had stayed behind and stopped to gab with Gramps in the hall. He had a special surprise for our precocious little sister, Donna, who was starring in her first Variety Show, and they were holding a confab on how to pop the surprise. Donna wasn't yet in school but Barb and I had added her to our sisters' act and also created her own solo, a Betty Boop song, for the tot.

Mrs. Minor shouted again, "I am the star!"

I met her anger with composure and my ultimate put-down.

"This is a kid's show."

She trembled with rage, but I continued, "Anyway, we were here first. These lockers aren't reserved. First come, first served." Drilled in the virtues of punctuality by our fireman father, we had arrived 45 minutes before show time and staked out our lockers.

Mrs. Minor lifted her hand and I thought she would strike me. I flinched, but only slightly, preparing for a blow, and then I heard Mom's voice.

When Mom had spied the chaos in the dressing room corner, she stalked right past Mrs. Minor to the spot where our costumes lay in a sad heap. She'd taken one took one look at the mess on the floor and went to work, digging in the locker and flinging all of Mrs. Minor's regalia across the room. Tap shoes and leotards were flying everywhere.

"What the hell is going on here?" she demanded. Deftly Mom had inserted herself between me and Mrs. Minor. I heaved a sigh of relief; Mom had my back.

Mrs. Minor blurted, "I am—" but Mom cut her off.

"Listen you has been. Who do you think you are? You look like an idiot prancing around half naked in a children's show. We come to see our kids."

Then Mom struck below the belt.

"Why don't you stop play acting? You are no chorus girl, honey. What's wrong with you anyway? Clomping around in a kids' show. You oughtta get your head examined."

Mrs. Minor began to object, "Now wait a minute. I am the choreographer of..." her voice trailed off as Mom poked a finger in her face.

"How dare you! Keep your mitts off my kids' costumes. I paid a lot of money to have them custom made. I didn't order them out of some cheap junk catalog. I've lived in this neighborhood for years and I support this school. I didn't give the Church all that money to let you push my kids around."

Mrs. Minor tried to object again, but Mom interrupted her, "You better not bother my kids again or I'll call the cops and I'll have you arrested. If I find out you bullied them again you will answer to me." Then Mom looked her up and down. "What is wrong with you anyway? Those legs of yours look like tree trunks and your hair is a rat's nest. You are too OLD for this show."

Someone must have tipped Father Shaughnessy off because he appeared suddenly in the doorway and intervened, trying to play peacemaker between the two women.

"Ladies, ladies, please. Calm down. This isn't the place for this. Think of the children."

But Mom wouldn't back down and she had a quick retort for the priest. "Listen, FATHER Shaughnessy (she drew his name out as she addressed him), Jack and I and all our relatives have been supporting this Church and school long before you were here and I'll be damned if I will let this harpy pick on my kids. I don't know what you brought her in for anyway. But I didn't spend the money to have costumes made to have this moron dump them on the floor."

Father Shaughnessy knew Mom should not be crossed. She was on a roll and there was no point in trying to reason with her. Still he tried to calm her, "Helen, we all appreciate what you and Jack do. I am sure it was just a misunderstanding." That didn't appease Mom.

"It was no misunderstanding. You keep this witch away from my kids."

Father Shaughnessy pulled Mrs. Minor aside and said a few words to her. Then he announced,

"There's some more locker space at the end of the hall. We'll make some room for you there, Margie."

Barbara and I winked and little Donna smirked as Mrs. Minor followed the priest out of the locker room and down the hall. Mrs. Minor had messed with the wrong person. Mom was like a tigress defending her young. We knew we would have nothing to worry about for the rest of the show. Mrs. Minor would never hassle us again.

We didn't understand how hard it might be to make a living giving dance lessons by the hour as a single woman with a child to support in the 1950s. There was no Mr. Minor. We couldn't guess that Mrs. Minor hoped to pick up some more dance pupils by advertising her studio.

For four nights I transformed myself into six-year-old Eloise and Mary was Nanny. Mom supplied Mary with her costume, but things tended to go missing in the Lennon house. Maybe Mitzy ate it. Or maybe Aidan was riding around with it in his fire truck. Anyway, when some part of her costume or props vanished, we'd improvise or Mom would pull another one of her fancy aprons out of the cupboard in the pantry. Somehow, we made it through each performance—thanks to Mom.

As we predicted, *Boogie Woogie Bugle Boy* was a favorite with the parents, grandparents, aunts and uncles who attended the show. They'd lived through the Great Depression, sacrificed during war years and served in the Armed Forces, so we, the next generation, could have idyllic childhoods. Barbara, Donna and I ran out on the stage and as we sang the first line, "He was a famous trumpet man from out Chicago way…" the audience erupted into applause and cheers. Some of the parents jitterbugged in the aisles. The Solick Sisters got a standing ovation every night of the show. Mom stood on the side beaming, singing along, and snapping her fingers to the beat of a song that she danced to when she was still a girl.

The audience went wild, laughing and cheering over our little blond sister, dressed as Betty Boop in a red satin flapper dress, tiny plastic high heels, headband, feather boa, and to complete the look, long, false eyelashes that Mom patiently applied before each show. Donna was the apple of Gramps' eye and he waited for the finale like a stage door Johnny with her favorite yellow roses and a big box of Fannie May candy for his darling granddaughter.

Mom wrapped her arms around the three of us. "You're my stars," Mom proclaimed. And she was ours, always there to protect and defend to make sure that we got our time to shine.

Liberty and Justice for All

If I Were 21 I'd Vote for Kennedy

Donna, my youngest sister, and I ascended the narrow staircase into my parents' attic. My feet hung over the tiny steps and I squeezed against the wall to make the turn and climb to the top of the steps. Donna warned me.

"You are not going to believe what I found."

"Remember how she said she threw everything away? Well—she didn't."

Dusty cardboard boxes covered the wooden floor of the space that ran the length of the bungalow. Garment racks held old clothing, uniforms, prom dresses, and evening wear. Dozens of Mom's wide-shouldered 80s suits from her days at Wells Lamont hung neatly in garment bags. The attic had always been off limits for us. Mom got mad when we tried to check it out and I hadn't been up there in years. I could still hear her nasal voice as I opened the creaky door from the kitchen to the attic

"Get outta there."

"There is nothing up there, what are you looking for?"

"Every time your sisters come over here, they walk out with something and I am sick of it."

When my eyes adjusted to the dim light provided by a single light bulb, I was amazed. It looked like the bargain basement in a department store. Donna guided me to a gift box wrapped with a ribbon. I opened it and made out old newspaper clippings and a familiar black and white photograph. The dates on the banner all read 1961. Mom had saved memorabilia from JFK's Presidential campaign. Donna and I carefully unfolded the yellowed pages. I wondered why Mom said she had thrown everything away. She used to say to us that if she had saved the campaign materials they would probably be worth a lot of money. Were the memories too painful for her? Was she trying to preserve a bit of her youthful idealism? Or did she think that she was preserving a bit of history for us.

She could not explain. Her nonstop banter had been silenced forever a few months. She'd suffered a subarachnoid hemorrhagic stroke while watching *Oprah*. When the neurologist told us that, even if she survived, she would never speak again, it made the decision easy. There would be no medical intervention. Mom lived to talk and I knew it was all over. I flew into Chicago to try and reach her before she died, but I felt on the plane that she was already gone. She officially died the next morning while I was on my way to her side. Now Donna and I could only speculate on her motives. She could be so contrary. But the news clippings also transported me to a street on Chicago's West Side when I was eleven years old and thought I could change the world.

"Kennedy, Kennedy—that's our cry. "

"K-E-N-N-E-D-Y!"

"Will he win it?"

"YES! YES! YES!"

"Kennedy, Kennedy—he's the best!"

I looked like a busker with my red coat with the raccoon collar festooned in campaign buttons. John F. Kennedy's and Lyndon B. Johnson's faces adorned the lapels. Barb danced alongside me with her blue and white pompoms, executing the cheers and occasionally flipping a cartwheel or handstand. Tiny Barb was the acrobat, dancer, and artist of the family. Smaller than all her classmates, popular and a great dancer, she was elected the captain of the grammar school cheerleaders in fifth grade. She learned all the cheers and moves from her black girlfriends.

As the neighborhood changed and people moved in and out, our school population changed, too. There were more black kids in Barb's class than mine, and all the girls immediately befriended Barb. Maybe it was because she was so small and sometimes bullies picked on her. Or maybe they just liked her dance moves. The girls were not Catholic and they had attended public school before moving to our neighborhood giving them an advantage in the cheers department. Barb picked up the dance moves quickly, and her diminutive size was a real advantage at the top of a human pyramid. Coats flapping in the October wind that swept the newspapers down the street to the end of the world, we marched up and down Madison Street with our placards, chanting the cheer at the top of our lungs. It was our mantra.

My buttons were my badge of courage and I wore them every day, only removing them when I entered my 7th grade classroom. Sister Francis Anne, my nemesis, was a Nixon supporter and forbade any campaign paraphernalia in her classroom. I could not believe it! I often asked myself was she really a Catholic or some demon sent from hell to torture me. I disliked her from the moment I walked into her classroom. Her threat set the tone for the year.

"I know what you kids did to your teacher last year and don't think for a minute you will get away with that in this classroom."

The middle aged nun peered out from her habit. Nothing escaped her notice even with those blinders. She wore glasses and a grim and steely expression. I had no idea how hold she really was—maybe my mother's age, maybe my grandmother's contemporary? I could not tell. Makeup had never seen this face. Sometimes a lock of hair would sneak out of the habit; I thought I spied some gray hairs. Sister was everywhere. Omnipresent, she patrolled the neighborhood after school and would call you out in class the next day if you ducked into a store to avoid her. I believed my time was my own after 3 p.m.; her surveillance was an invasion of my privacy. I would not give her obeisance during my playtime, so I often faced her wrath the following day.

From the first day of school, my sense of justice was offended by Sister's attempts to organize the students and make learning a competition. Our inner city school was very diverse and most of the neighborhood children, even non-Catholics, attended the school if the parents could afford the $1 tuition charge per child monthly. Children of all ethnicities, children with profound hearing loss, and children with cerebral palsy—all attended St. Mel's. Those blue serge uniforms made us all seem like equals, but as I got older and visited friends at home, I had begun to realize that we did not all have the same advantages. Some kids had a lot less; some kids parents worked in the factories at night and they were alone; some kids' parents had abandoned them; some were just poor; some kids' parents did not speak English; some kids only had their school uniforms to wear.

So when Sister proclaimed her methodology on the first day of school, I was incensed. Product of a Catholic school I knew injustice when I saw it - she was unfair and mean. Weekly, she declared, she would publish a seating chart based on the previous week's grades. The smartest child would have the first row, first seat, and so on. We would all compete for our placement. I knew I would be in the first row, but I could only imagine how bad the kid in the last row, last seat would feel. I thought it was a rotten idea.

I was never afraid of Sister Francis Anne, I knew my parents would also back me up if we crossed swords, and I always got good grades. But I knew better than to mess with her. She whipped kids with a ruler on a regular basis and was known to send kids flying into the walls if they displeased her. I saw no reason to acquire any more childhood scars and removed my precious buttons and shoved them in my coat pockets until school let out.

Since the rumors of a young Catholic Senator running for the Presidency had surfaced, I had identified with underdog Jack Kennedy. My pious Italian aunt Camille cried when she found anti-Catholic literature in her mailbox. It seemed like a personal attack to her. She brought it to my mom who pronounced it "Propaganda" and "Idiotic." The crudely drawn cartoon depicted Senator Kennedy sitting on the Pope's lap. It read, "Big John and Little John." I realized they meant Pope John XXIII. He seemed like a nice guy and all but I questioned what he had to do with any election in the United States. I thought the Pope was busy with ecumenism and guitar masses. I figured whoever drew it did not know any Catholics. It seemed ridiculous to me and I, too, took it personally.

Jack Kennedy was a hero after all. I read about Kennedy's heroism in World War II and thought I probably could have done the same if I had been a better swimmer. I actually did not see the difference between a skinny eleven-year-old girl growing up in the Chicago's West Side slum and a wealthy young politician from Massachusetts. I knew we had had a lot in common. We were both Catholic; although I had decided I was an atheist. Our ancestors came from Ireland. And, after all, I reasoned, we might even be related. Grandma's maiden name was FitzGerald.

Everyone in my family was crazy for JFK, the first Catholic who really seemed to have a chance in his bid for the Presidency. My mother hung pictures of him in the window of our apartment and around the house. Dad said he could not wear them on his fireman's uniform and they got into an argument about it. Mom watched every broadcast about JFK and idolized his wife, Jackie, promptly adopting the bouffant hairdo and pillbox hat that was the uniform of female Kennedy devotees. My mother's sister, Aunt Alice, mother of ten children, campaigned hard for Kennedy in the conservative state of Washington. We felt a personal connection with the candidate when Aunt Alice sent a picture of her shaking hands with Senator Kennedy. Maybe that's where I first got the idea to volunteer for the campaign. Kennedy's call to action resonated with me. I enlisted my younger sister, Barb, who was conscripted to participate in all my adventures.

"I want to volunteer for Kennedy."

"Do you think Mom will let us?"

"Are you kidding? She loves Kennedy as much as Daddy."

"You better ask her."

I decided the best approach was to simply inform Mom that we would be volunteering. I had been an unpaid worker at school for many causes. I appeared in the variety show, donated money for the missions in Africa, sold Catholic newspaper subscriptions in the annual drive, played games with the residents of the school for kids with developmental disabilities, and went to visit the orphanage. Every year some nun would draft me to help clean up the classrooms and halls before school opened. This was just a logical next step for me. We were learning about government and I wanted to get involved. Mom was always writing letters to the editor that she put on top of the fridge and forgot to mail. She helped tutor the Puerto

Rican kids in English even though she couldn't speak Spanish, so I was pretty sure she would agree.

As predicted, she was wildly enthusiastic. Going downtown would not be an option for her. Stuck at home with the Babies, she could live vicariously through her eleven and nine year old daughters. She urged us to bypass the local office, go straight to the top, and head for the campaign office on Michigan Avenue to offer our services. She even coached us on what to say when we presented ourselves as volunteers. We were ecstatic and marched up and down the long hall in our apartment, singing campaign songs. We decided to head down there the next weekend. We couldn't wait for Saturday.

Barb and I carefully planned our expedition to downtown Chicago. We decided that this was serious business and we needed to look professional, meaning older. Saturday, we got up early, ate our bowls of Frosted Flakes, and dressed in our best clothes. We did not even turn on the TV. We'd already agreed we would skip the movies on Saturday until Kennedy was elected. I was 5'2" and 75 pounds; Barb was a least a foot shorter than me. When I looked in the mirror, I thought I looked like the Scarecrow and Barb like a munchkin. I knew we had a lot of work to do to make ourselves look more mature. I had enormous feet for an eleven-year-old and had a hard time finding dress shoes, but my grandma had discovered a shoe outlet in the country where they could fit me.

I carefully selected the black suede pumps with half inch heels and my best white socks. I picked out a nice plaid shirtwaist dress that I would wear to church, my good coat, and a scarf. I really felt like I was doing something important. I was going to change the world. I advised Barb on her outfit, although I knew she had impeccable taste for a nine-year-old girl. I thought she looked stunning in her blue wool princess waist double breasted coat trimmed in velvet. Before we left, we surveyed ourselves in the mirror in the front hall, and decided we looked every bit like campaign workers. Then, we gave Mom a kiss and ran down the three flights of stairs to the street and to our destiny. We waved to Mom as she watched us from the 3rd story apartment window before we boarded the Madison Street bus.

The bus brakes screeched as we stopped on the corner. Barb and I had our fare and figured we had enough money to buy something to eat at Walgreen's cafeteria, if we got a break. The little leather wrist coin purses that our Aunt Alice made for us when she was in the sanitarium recovering from tuberculosis each held $1, the allowance we spent at the Saturday movies. We boarded and dropped our quarters in the box. We did not get a transfer; we wanted to save the nickel. The green and yellow CTA bus took us straight to the Loop down Madison Street —past lush Garfield Park, past the brownstones that had once been grand residences with ballrooms on the top floor, now boarding houses and apartments, past blocks and blocks of idle, sad men sitting on the curbs on Skid Row, past the cheap liquor stores with the garish signs advertising exotic brews like MD 20-20 and Thunderbird, and passed flophouses and bars.

Although the trip was really only five miles, it was all a great adventure to me. Skid Row was just another cityscape to me; our gramps, a recovering alcoholic, had explained all about what it was like to be on Skid Row on one of our many shopping trips with him. Finally, the bus crossed the river and we were in the Loop. I was so excited. The skyscrapers and department stores felt like sheltering arms to me. I felt like we belonged there. When the bus reached Michigan Avenue, we pulled the cord to signal our stop and got off.

To save our cash we had decided to walk the rest of the way. A chilly wind off Lake Michigan blew our hair and made our noses runny and red. We huddled close together and hugged the lovely shops and offices that lined Michigan Avenue to keep away the cold. Finally we reached campaign headquarters. Banners decorated the storefront windows. Jack Kennedy and Lyndon Johnson smiled down at us—their newest campaign volunteers.

We presented ourselves to the receptionist at the front desk. I told the young woman in the bouffant hairdo and pink A-line dress, "We support Senator Kennedy and we want to help." The young woman smiled and asked us to take a seat. We looked around the big open campaign war room filled with mismatched industrial metal desks and chairs of various shapes and sizes. Phones were ringing and young volunteers were staffing the phones or kibitzing in corners. She called someone and, in a few minutes, an older woman greeted us. She asked us to accompany her to a small office for an interview.

"Hello girls and welcome."

"What are your names?"

"Anita and Barbara Solick"

"Our mother's maiden name is McMahon and my grandma's name was FitzGerald."

The woman smiled.

"So you want to volunteer?"

"Yes, ma'am."

"How old are you girls?"

"Eleven, almost twelve, and nine almost ten."

"Where do you go to school?"

"St. Mel–Holy Ghost School"

"Did you come here by yourself?"

"Yes, we took the bus."

I thought her eyebrow rose a bit, but she recovered.

"That is a good school."

"Well, girls, we've got plenty for you to do."

We passed. We were in! And to their credit the campaign staffers never patronized us or laughed at us, although their young volunteers probably cut comical figures. They took us seriously, treating us with the same respect they gave to the adult volunteers. We were installed at one of the industrial desks just like the adults. Armed with office supplies including an amazing invention—a wet sponge to help with sealing envelopes, we got busy addressing envelopes and stamping mailings. The office manager even let us file and look up addresses in the telephone book. She would check on us periodically and tell us when to take breaks, but pretty soon we were trusted to just do the work. When we ran out of things to do we would ask for more. Eventually, I would answer the telephone if the adults were really busy. In the evening, when we finished our work, we would ask someone for campaign materials to take home and trudged back to catch the Madison Street bus with our arms full.

And, we continued our efforts in the Madison Crawford Business District. Barb and I leafleted the entire neighborhood. We stuck the materials on street lights and in the abandoned newsstands. We handed them to shoppers. When we ran out of posters, we made our own on construction paper. I created the slogans and Barb did the artwork. We used my little rubber printing press letters to set the type. We went to all the stores in the neighborhood and I badgered the merchants to put Kennedy posters in the windows. We hit them all, store after store along Madison Street—the bakery, the Greek grocers, the pawn shop, the funeral parlors, the fortune teller, Personnel Liquors, the butcher shop, and the A & P. Most of the smaller merchants agreed to put the posters in the window, but I considered it a real coup when the Market Basket manager agreed. After school, we walked Madison Street carrying posters and chanting the Kennedy cheer.

Every Saturday until the election Barb and I took the bus downtown to work at campaign headquarters. I tried to follow the election issues and scoured the daily paper for any information about how the campaign was going and any indication that we would win. It was my campaign now. I was licking envelopes when we heard the exciting news. The office manager told me that Jack Kennedy would be making a stop in Chicago. I was jubilant. I could go see him. Maybe I could get an autograph.

We went downtown when Jack and Bobby made an appearance with Mayor Daley. People lined the streets. The crowds were oppressive and I felt dwarfed. Still I was determined to get a look at Jack Kennedy. I told Barb to hold my hand tight and we started to weave our way through the masses. I felt claustrophobic but I pressed on. I could smell the wool coats, perfume, aftershave, hair spray, beer, spaghetti lunch, cigarettes, and asphalt. Someone stepped on my foot, and elbowed me in the ribs, but I pressed on. Finally, I saw the stand and podium. There was a small break in the crowd and Barb and I and managed to sneak under the ropes that kept the public back. We ran up to John and Bobby. Suddenly, I froze; I was speechless. I didn't know what to say to my idol. I blurted out a greeting.

"Hi Senator Kennedy, we volunteer for you."

Bobby smiled and I was sure Jack was about to say something when I heard a shout.

"Hey you girls, get yourselves back behind those ropes."

With that a burly policeman grabbed us both by the coat collars and escorted us back to the designated area for the public. He warned us to stay behind the ropes. But I didn't care; I had seen Jack and Bobby Kennedy up close. I was mad at myself that I did not have a pen and did not get an autograph, but I had still seen him. When we got home and told our mother, she congratulated us and regaled us with stories of how she climbed down a fire escape and played hooky from high school to see Frank Sinatra when he was appearing in Chicago. And when I returned to school on Monday, I told everyone that I met Senator Kennedy.

The race was neck and neck. I tried to debate the campaign issues with my classmates who did their best to ignore me. Then the debates were announced. I nervously checked the TV listings in the *Chicago Tribune* daily to make sure I did not miss them. Then the big day arrived. I watched the first Kennedy–Nixon debate. Senator Kennedy was handsome and inspiring. Vice President Nixon was, well, old, nervous, and sweaty looking. He looked creepy to me. My grandfather was younger and better looking. I was no psychic, but I knew it was over for Nixon.

Our last Saturday at campaign headquarters was a little sad for me. I didn't want it to end. I worked the entire day and at end of the day, the office manager and other volunteers gathered around to thank us. They told Barb and me we were making history. We packed up the materials and cleaned our shared desk and said our goodbyes and wished everyone good luck. It felt anticlimactic to me as we rode the bus home in the evening. Spending Saturday at the movies was never going to top this experience.

Election Day was like a holy day for us. Daddy went to vote when the polls opened. He had to get to work. Mom had her hair done, dressed up, and put on makeup for the occasion. She had a neighbor watch the Babies after we got home from school and told us we could go with her to the polling place in the little grocery store on Keeler. When we got to the polling place, Mom spied two ward heelers trying to influence voters. They offered her 5 bucks to vote the Republican ticket. Almost combative, she was like a tigress and pounced on them. They knew her reputation for a sharp tongue and wit and drew back from the door when she confronted them.

"Hey you crooks, you are supposed to be fifty feet from the polling place."

"Get back where you belong, this is a democracy."

"I am going to report you to the election commission."

The men moved away from the store until Mom cast her vote. She marched in to the polling place and told the staffers that they better keep an eye on those crooks outside. We waited while she went behind the curtains and then she came out and deposited her ballot. Now we just had to wait. As we walked across the alley to return to our apartment, my mother reminded us how it was a privilege to vote and how her ancestors and our dad had fought for our freedom. I asked Mom why she did not just take the 5 bucks from the cronies outside the polling place and vote the way she wanted. I thought they would never know.

"It would be dishonest. Then I'd be like those crooks."

It was down to the wire in the polls, however, and I waited nervously for the election results. Daddy was at the firehouse. Mom let Barb and I stay up late to watch the returns on TV. We sat up with her, eating M&Ms and drinking Cokes. Her hair wrapped in toilet paper to preserve her bouffant, Mom smoked one Lucky Strike after another and I bit my nails except when Mom yelled at me to stop. Sometimes she would talk back to the TV as the states reported their returns. Finally, when it looked like Kennedy had won, we went to bed, and dreamt of celebrations and being invited to the Inauguration Ball.

The next day, when the results were in and Nixon had conceded, I rejoiced. We had won. I could not wait to get to school. I ran all the way, yelling and cheering. But a big surprise awaited me when I walked into Room 21. Sister Francis Anne was on a rampage. Furious at Nixon's defeat, she tore the classroom apart, dumping everything in front of her desk. She ran through the cloakroom, yanking coats off the hooks and dumping boots in the middle of the floor. She even took the books that my dad had donated to the classroom from the bookshelf in the back of the room and threw them over the heads of the students. I was insulted. The only thing she didn't throw was the statue of the Blessed Virgin that stood in the corner of the room, looking on in dismay. She castigated the class screaming, "Look at the mess you made. You will clean it up."

The boys, who were used to her tirades and violent outbursts, began laughing at her, which only infuriated her more. The other girls scurried to pick up the mess and put the room in order. In defiance, I would not budge. She glared at me.

"Anita Solick, get up."

"No, Sister, I won't. I didn't do this; you did and I am not cleaning it up."

"Young lady, don't you talk back to me—ten demerits!"

Then she turned and hit one of the bigger boys who had the misfortune of being seated in the third row first seat on his head with a book and his nose started to bleed. I felt like I was responsible and felt bad for him. But he just snickered and muttered.

"You lose, Sister."

Sister Francis Anne raged all day and I had to stay after school and write one thousand times, "I must be kind to Sister and my classmates." I breezed through the punishment. Kennedy and I had won and there was nothing that could dampen my spirits, not even old Sister Francis Anne. I had elected a President.

The Upside Down Year

Was it me? Or was it everybody else? At twelve going on thirteen, I wrestled to understand myself and the changes that were going on around me. *Mad Magazine* had proclaimed it so and 1961 definitely felt like an upside-down year to me.

The year started out very well for me when Jack Kennedy was inaugurated. My younger sister Barbara and I volunteered with Kennedy's election campaign and I watched the young President take his oath of office. I was personally excited by the prospect of transformation and his words as he called the nation to service in his inaugural address.

But my euphoria was short-lived. Daily, the *Chicago Tribune* headlines shouted the news of a world in tumult. The United States severed relations with Cuba, Patrice Lumumba was assassinated, and the Bay of Pigs was a failure. The Cold War raged and plans on how to build a bomb shelter were published in the paper. There were air raid drills. I examined the map that the *Trib* published detailing the devastation if an A bomb were dropped on Chicago and made a plan. Unable to tolerate a blanket when I slept, I knew I would not like to be trapped under a pile of bricks in the restaurant basement. I read books about the devastation after Nagasaki and Hiroshima and I knew what I must do. I secretly plotted to run in the street if the air raid was real and become a shadow on the sidewalk.

While 1961 offered some glimmers of hope, like Kennedy's establishment of the Peace Corps, every day brought ominous news that frightened or disturbed me. I worried about whether I would live to be eighteen. It seemed a long way off.

In my small corner of the universe at Madison and Keeler, the world was changing, too. My neighborhood had been in transition all through the 1950s, and, for the first time, Black and Puerto Rican families settled in our neighborhood and integrated our school. The topic of conversation with the adults always seemed to turn to integration, property values and fears that the neighborhood would turn into a slum. Adults used phrases like "the colored" or worse when they talked about my classmates and friends and their families.

It was an awkward time for me and no one noticed it more painfully than I did. I was younger than the rest of my classmates, prepubescent, but precocious. While some kids who had not yet entered the chaos of adolescence played on, unaware of the pain and ecstasy that awaited them, I had a mature head on a small body, and, saw it all ahead of me. I read voraciously—maybe that was my problem. I'd read all the new releases Dad brought home from Bantam Books for me. I made short work of *Franny and Zooey* and decided I would eat nothing but cheeseburgers and Cokes. *The Carpetbaggers* held no interest for me; it was too long to sustain my attention, even if it was a potboiler with steamy passages. My curiosity about sex could not be satiated by steamy best-sellers but I was too young and gawky to experiment.

When I looked around me I saw my friends becoming young women. But I still saw a skinny child in the mirror, with too short hair. I wanted to look like Audrey Hepburn, but with that cowlick I thought I resembled Alfalfa.

It was still warm and brilliantly sunny that first day of school in September 1961. The leaves had not yet started to turn, but I felt that crispness in the wind that whispered of fall soon to come. In eighth grade students were to prepare for high school and that meant a new uniform. I was grateful that hot day to trade in the old blue serge jumper, shiny from wear, for a blue skirt and white blouse.

I surveyed myself in the mirror of the dresser I shared with Barbara. The reflection had its drawbacks. I was so skinny that the uniform blouse collar gaped around my neck. The red nylon scarf, branding me as an eighth grader, hung loosely under the collar, like a yoke around an emaciated horse. I tried to tie the scarf tighter to take up the slack, but the collar bunched up. The Elizabethan look was not going to be acceptable to the nuns, so I left the collar and scarf slack.

I thought I looked like I was wearing someone else's clothes. I smiled. My eyes and teeth looked to me to be too big for my long face. The short cut of my dark brown hair seemed to exaggerate this effect. Most aggravating to me was the cowlick that kept my thick bangs from staying flat on my brow. No matter what I did the night before to try and calm the beast—tape, hair spray, and Dippity Do smeared like wallpaper paste on my forehead—the infuriating cowlick always won the battle. Dismayed, I decided to give up and head to school.

The first week of school was lost in a lot of administrative officialdom. Announcements from the principal, Sister Veronica Ann, rang out over the public address system. Eighth graders were given a homeroom teacher and would rotate classes with assigned groups for English, Math, Science, and History. This new arrangement was supposed to prepare us for the high school environment.

My homeroom teacher was Sister Bernard—a tall thin, tomboyish young woman who wore wire-rimmed glasses. Enthusiastic and athletic, she would need every ounce of energy she could muster that year with a homeroom of 62 boys and three girls. The nun thrived on challenge and had a special place in her heart for the students who struggled most with their studies. One of the vanguard—a new breed of nuns, socially committed, working in depressed communities— more confidante than disciplinarian, she encouraged her students to think and to ask questions. I had a million of them.

Sister Bernard liked to get the children involved. The first day of class she ticked off a list of volunteer opportunities, and a reward system for participation.

"Class, I'd like your attention. There are many areas where St. Mel's and the community need your help. I'll have a signup sheet at the front of the room and you can earn merits for your participation."

My ears pricked up. I expected to rack up a few demerits that year and thought I would hedge my bets and avoid detention by signing up for as many activities as possible. Besides, I enjoyed volunteering and the notion of me, a young girl, being able to make a difference really appealed to me.

After school, Mary Lennon, Ray Gerardi and Michael Gaffney walked home via Monroe Street. Mary and I had become friendly with the two boys, who were seminary-bound after eighth grade, when we walked the same route after school. They both had a vocation, which made them seem sort of neutral to adolescent girls and worthy of our confidence. We'd stroll home after class, gossiping and complaining about friends, schoolmates, and classes.

"Are you going to the sock hop they announced at school today?" Mary asked the two boys.

Ray piped up, "Why not?"

"Well I thought maybe since you are going to be a priest…"

"Hey, I am only thirteen, I'm not dead yet!"

We all laughed, at thirteen, death, like being eighteen, seemed a long way off.

Once back in my apartment on Madison Street, I gave Mom the rundown on the day's events.

Her eyes lit up when I mentioned the sock hop. Mom loved dancing and fancied herself a great dancer. I had to admit she was pretty good.

She leapt up from the kitchen chair and announced, "I'm going to teach you the latest dance. All the jet setters are doing it. It's called the Twist."

Barb and I groaned and rolled our eyes. The Twist was last year's fad. If Mom was doing it, we knew it was really passé.

"Mom, nooo. No one does that dance anymore. Only old people."

"No, you girls are wrong. Frank Sinatra and the jet setters do it, and Andy Williams does it. I saw it on TV. Look, watch me. Here is how you do it. Round and round and up and down." Mom gyrated in her housecoat demonstrating her best moves.

"Mom, exactly. Frank Sinatra is old."

"Girls, the bobby soxers all loved Frank when I was in high school. I climbed out a window of Providence High School to go see him. The girls all swooned over him"

"Mom, yeah, we know. That was a long time ago."

Mom was then thirty-seven.

To further my righteous pre-teen chagrin, the news delivered by Sister Bernard that week dealt an unexpected blow.

"Can't you find some other mom?"

"Anita, your mother said she wanted to help and this is where we have the greatest need. We need an English tutor for the Spanish-speaking children."

The Lives of the Saints and a bloody martyrdom for the nun flashed through my mind, when, over my strenuous objections, she asked my mother to volunteer tutoring the new students from Puerto Rico in English.

"Sister Bernard, how could you?" She should die like Saint Agnes; I'll yank out her ribs myself. I groaned. A budding adolescent, I was fiercely protective of my privacy. I had little enough of it as it was living with three younger siblings and only one block from school. I did not want my mother hanging around all day, spying on me. I wanted the classroom to be my separate place, away from parental expectations. But Sister Bernard had a nose for another do-gooder like herself and soon, although she did not speak Spanish, Mom was installed in the cloakroom, tutoring the kids several times a week. She connected with the kids, especially the boy. He loved baseball and so did Mom. Using comic books and baseball magazines she purchased herself, Mom proved an able tutor, and soon the kids were speaking their first English phrases. An advocate for higher education, she pushed them to think about high school and college, and helped one of the girls, who had been destined for a young marriage, to secure a scholarship to Providence High School, Mom's alma mater.

By nature I was a child who questioned authority and I began to feel even more skeptical about the status quo. When the orientation for Sacristy custodians was announced, I was interested. At last I would have a look at the inner sanctum behind the altar where the priest donned his vestments and prepared for the Holy Sacrament of

Mass. Girls could not serve at Mass; there were only altar boys then. I imagined being initiated into ancient secret rituals. As it turned out, there were no secret rituals and no custody of precious relics. Sister Petronella told us we would be allowed access to clean, dust, vacuum, and wash the floors, and this was a great honor. She began to show us around the ante room, but I interrupted.

The young feminist in me was outraged. I sputtered, "Why? I don't even do this at home. You mean want us to be maids?"

Truth was, Mom didn't like housework or anything to do with homemaking and she had taught me well. We argued over my doing chores around the house and I was usually derelict in my duties. I'd had many a screaming fight with Mom about housework. I wasn't about to sign on for more. Why didn't they have boys cleaning up after themselves? And I didn't know those priest smoked cigarettes!

Sister shushed me with just a look and I said nothing more. When we left the chapel, I announced to my friends that I was not a cleaning lady and wouldn't be going back. I told them I thought it was unfair. In my mind, I questioned the nun's role and wondered how she felt about being assigned clean-up duty.

Until then, I thought of the nuns as authority figures in the Church who had a good life. They ruled the school with iron hands. Even as a small girl, I could see the priests had a lot more freedom and perks, riding around in Cadillacs, getting free meals at all the restaurants, ski vacations and boats at their disposal and questioned the disparity. But Mom said the nuns had it made—many came from large, poor, Catholic families and would never have had the money to go to college. In exchange for a life of service, they got an education and meals and lodging for free. They never paid for anything. They were taken care of for life.

Now—I could not imagine teaching a bunch of bratty kids all day, but I thought Mom had a point. And Mom was not big on marriage and family. In fact, she never said anything to us about getting married and having children. She talked about where we would go to college and our careers, but never marriage. I grew up thinking the convent wasn't such a bad deal, but now I had my doubts. What kind of an honor was it to clean up after a bunch of sloppy men and some boys? I stormed out of the sacristy and told my friends I would never be back for more.

Planning for the dance interested me more, although I had already determined I would not be sticking around for the clean-up committee. I decided I would help organize the committees and volunteered to recruit the volunteers. I pictured myself as more of an executive type anyway. I drafted a list of committees and posted a handwritten sign-up sheet with a brief description of responsibilities at the front of the room.

Copping a line from my President, JFK, I made a pitch to my homeroom, urging the students to give back to the school and to ask their parents to participate as chaperones. I asked for five people to sign up for each committee. Sister Bernard added an incentive by promising 10 merits for anyone who signed up, so I got plenty of volunteers.

At that moment, a tall figure in sun glasses swaggered into our homeroom, snapping his fingers. "Duke, Duke, Duke, Duke of Earl, Duke, Duke, Duke of Earl…" John "The Duke of Earl" Lee heralded his arrival every day with a serenade for Room 21. The class broke into laughter and applause, as Sister Bernard put a halt to his signature song with, "Mr. Lee, take off those sunglasses and take your seat."

Block by block, our neighborhood was becoming integrated. The Civil Rights movement was the national topic of conversation and our neighborhood was no exception. And while parents may have seethed about integration and its impact, their children were more accepting.

John Earl Lee was one of three black students—one boy and two girls—that joined my homeroom that year. Towering over the rest of the students, John Earl Lee immediately established his reputation as King of the Cool, the classroom comic, and a favorite of teachers and students alike. His knack for impersonations cracked us up. Instantly popular, he hung out with the hip kids, the kids who barely acknowledged my existence. By contrast, the two girls, Anne and Rhonda were serious types who excelled at their studies, and they fit right in too, making friends with the other "smart" kids.

Barbara's class, two years behind mine, welcomed many more minority students, mostly black and biracial students. All Baptists, they were excused from religion class unless they exhibited an interest. Instead, they went to breakout classes. I fantasized about what they were doing. After nine years of study, memorizing catechism was not my favorite subject. St. Mel's Church, hoping to rope in some converts, would sweeten the deal for non-Catholics and offer a discount on tuition if the families attended Sunday Mass where the priests would peddle salvation. Amazingly, many families took advantage of the offer, attending both Mass and the Baptist services on Sundays.

Barb became good friends with most of the black girls when they all tried out for cheerleading. Barb's new friends had attended public school before coming to St. Mel's and they knew all the latest cheers. She was so tiny and athletic that she was instantly selected for the squad. Because of her size, she was the perfect choice to top the human pyramid—so easy to hold her up! The black girls befriended my sometimes shy little sister, taught her all the hot routines, and elected her captain of the team. Barb was blossoming and developing her own circle of pals.

And, while adults fretted about declining property values, blockbusters, and the impact of integration on their neighborhood, the kids were indifferent to their fears. All we could think about was the big dance.

I knew Mom would let me buy a new outfit to wear. I had my eye on a pleated skirt and a mohair sweater in the showcase in front of Madigan's Department Store and I was sure I could persuade her to buy it for me. Or maybe Gram and Gramps would get it for me. I thought the bulky mohair sweater would make me look less skinny.

The sock hop committees were meeting after school several times a week and would report back to the Executive Committee. Plans were going well, I thought, and I hung around after school one day to fill Sister Bernard in on our progress. Very officious, I'd prepared a report on the little Remington portable typewriter my parents had given me for a Christmas present the year before. Sister Bernard listened to my report, but she seemed more distracted than usual.

"Ah, Anita, I wanted to let you know that we will be having some guests at the sock hop."

"Oh really, who, Sister? Bishop Hillinger? The Cardinal? "

"No, no, nobody like that. We are going to have some students from neighboring schools attending the dance."

"You mean the kids from Tilton? Sister, we are going to need a lot more chairs and refreshments."

"No, not exactly. Well, some of the guests attend Tilton, but there won't be that many. We've told the Negro students that they may bring guests to the sock hop. They will be bringing friends from other schools."

"OK, well, can anyone bring a friend, because I need to know what the headcount will be."

She hesitated, "No, only the Negro students will be bringing friends."

"I don't understand." I thought maybe this was another thinly disguised effort to recruit Catholics, but Sister Bernard set me straight.

"We told the Negro students they could bring friends, because we were concerned that no one would dance with them."

"Now I really don't get it."

They are the best dancers in the school, I thought. They know all the new dances. Why wouldn't people want to dance with them? I know why they don't want to dance with me. I am not a good dancer, I have big feet, and I am a brain. But why not them?"

Sister Bernard sighed and explained, "Because they are Negroes."

"Sister, I don't think so. Those kids know the latest dances from their old school. They've been showing us in the playground. You are wrong."

"Well, the decision has been made, so add three more to your count of attendees."

After school, when I told Mom about my conversation with Sister Bernard, she brushed it off with, "Some parents must have complained to the school. They'd throw a fit if they find out their kid was dancing with a colored kid."

Then she told me something she'd never mentioned before.

"You know, when I was young, most of the men were at war, but Negroes weren't yet allowed to serve in the military. The men registered but they were passed over by the Selective Service

Boards. All our boyfriends had shipped overseas, and, well you know how I love to dance. So we girls would head to the south side clubs to go jitterbugging. These clubs were all owned by colored people. They had the best music and dancers. Sometimes, some big stars even showed up, like Billie Holiday or Lena Horne. The Negro men came dressed to the nines; lots of them wore zoot suits. They'd ask the white girls to dance, especially me because I was the best, and we'd jitterbug until the wee hours. There were some great dancers there; I picked up a lot of new steps. But we couldn't tell anyone and they could never come to the white clubs. It was taboo. If anyone had found out we would have been in trouble. And the guys risked getting beat up or worse by dancing with us."

"What? Doesn't seem very fair. If someone wants to dance."

"You don't understand. Men were fighting and dying to make the world safe. There was resentment."

"Well, it wasn't their fault if they weren't allowed in the Army, was it?"

"Yes, well, people were prejudiced and Truman changed that. A lot of things are changing, but some people aren't ready for it. They feel threatened."

"Mom, I don't get it, these kids are our friends. Why would anyone feel threatened by them? They are kids."

Mom cut right to the chase. "It's a long story. People are afraid of anything they are unfamiliar with. Maybe they're afraid if kids get too friendly they will marry their children and their grandchildren will be black."

"Oh, Mom, nobody wants to get married. We want to dance. Anyway, some of Barb's friends' parents are negro and white, so the girls are both."

"People call them mulattos. And that's what I am talking about. Those girls will never be accepted by either Negroes or whites." Mom sighed, "They are pretty girls."

"What, Mom, that's stupid. Why not? Yolanda and her sister, Barb J—they are the cutest girls in her class and the best cheerleaders."

"That's the way it is now, honey. People are not ready for it."

"Well, Mom. You can't stop progress."

This conversation had a profound effect on me; a curtain parted; I wasn't a child anymore. At once, I saw the inequities, the cruelty, and the sexism—everything that seemed to be holding us humans back from being the best we could be. I felt sad and angry. I wanted my classmates to bring their friends—all of them. I wanted everyone to be welcomed at our dance. My enthusiasm dampened for the sock hop, but I went on, if half-heartedly, performing my volunteer duties... I never made promises I didn't keep, but I did not care as much about the dance.

The night of the dance arrived. Mary Lennon and I agreed we'd walk together as usual to the school that night. Mom gave us the final once-over before we headed off for the dance. She retied the scarf Mary wore around her neck, and smoothed my unruly bangs.

"You both look terrific."

I knew we must because Mom did not hand out compliments easily. You had to earn them.

Dad looked up from Peter Gunn. He beamed and motioned me over for a peck on the cheek. "You look beautiful, honey. Have fun. Don't let Sister Mary Holy Water give you a hard time."

Dad never like nuns and called all our teachers, "Sister Mary Holy Water."

"Daddy, her name is Sister Bernard."

Dad shot me a mischievous grin, "Oh right, right. Have fun."

That night the weather was cooler and my pink mohair sweater was not too warm as Mary and I walked to school before the dance. I wore a crystal necklace that Gramps bought for me and I thought I looked grown up. It was getting dark earlier now and as we hurried along Madison Street towards the school, I saw a big yellow harvest moon rising in the sky. Indian summer was usually one of my favorite times, but that night, I felt discontent growing in me. Things seemed off.

"I hope everything goes okay tonight. I spent a lot of time on the planning."

Mary, who had inherited her mother's easy-going manner, tried to reassure me. "It'll all be fine."

As we turned on Washington, we saw the school lights were all on and the doors wide open. Parents stood in the vestibule, running interference for the nuns, checking students out and directing them to the basement of the school. Mary and I headed downstairs to the basement meeting room, called Sodality Hall. The committees were putting the finishing touches on the lunchroom which served as our ballroom that night. The decorating committee had done a great job transforming the room with paper streamers, balloons and banners with glitter that read, "Welcome, St. Mel's Class of 1962." I took one last look and decided we were as ready as we'd ever be.

Students arrived in pairs and groups. When the room was full, Sister Veronica Ann called us to attention. She never missed a chance to kick off an event and give a speech.

"Young ladies and gentlemen—your attention, please! There will be no close dancing. Gentlemen, you must stay an arm's length from your partner. Young ladies, there will be one Ladies Choice dance tonight. I will announce when you may ask someone to dance with you. There will be no leaving the dance tonight. Anyone who leaves the dance will not be permitted to reenter. If you are chewing gum, please spit it out in a napkin and dispose of it in the trash receptacle. We will have no gum on this beautiful linoleum floor. If I smell smoke on any of you boys, you will be ejected and sent home. Let the dance begin."

Then someone dropped the needle on the record player and the thunk rang out over the public address system which had been jerry-rigged to serve as an amplifier by Ray, who also handled the audiovisual requests for our homeroom. I thought he was an electrical genius. The first song was "Michael Row the Boat Ashore". I suspected this was Sister Veronica Ann's choice. She needn't have worried about kids getting too close. The kids just stood around and looked at one another. The black students all stood in a corner, talking with their dates. I felt inner terror—the sock hop was going to bomb. It would be a failure. All my hard work down the drain!

Mercifully, songs were only two minutes 13 seconds long then and Michael rowed his boat to shore quickly. My friend Ray took matters in hand. He grabbed a new 45 by Gary U.S. Bonds and plopped it on the spindle.

The song was like an anthem. "Well, doncha know that I danced, I danced 'til a quarter to three…"

Someone let out a scream and everyone crowded the floor. Kids danced in a circle, they danced by themselves, they danced in a line. No one danced with a partner; we danced as if we were one person. Black and white and Puerto Rican, all celebrating our youth and our love of rock and roll. The mohair sweater stuck to my spine, my cowlick popped up with the humidity, and the garter belt that held up my stockings dug into my bony thigh, but I didn't care. I was in ecstasy; the sock hop was a success!

Ray played joyous song after joyous song. "Tossin' and Turnin'", "Runaway", "Hit the Road Jack", the "Bristol Stomp" and "Shop Around". My fears receded with each note and I thought of something I'd heard a jazz musician say, "Music is a country where there is no color." It might have been an upside-down year, but I felt like it had flipped over to the A side that night.

Ms. Solick for President

It seems like hubris to me now, but I actually thought I could win the 8th grade class election because John F. Kennedy won the Presidency. I volunteered for Kennedy's campaign in 7th grade, and he won. I'd elected a U.S. President.

So, the following year when the class election was announced, I figured this was my time. After all, I was an old hand at running a campaign. When we returned to school in September, my home room teacher, lanky, tomboy Sister Bernard, made the big announcement in class—nominations would be accepted in one week. The President and Vice President would lead all four classrooms and represent St. Mel-Holy Ghost School. At what, I wondered, but did not then ask.

I thought I was the obvious choice. I was certain I was qualified and had demonstrated leadership. I'd been top in my class for several years now and volunteered for many school activities. I was a star of the annual variety show. And, I had real campaign experience.

As we walked home from school, kicking the fall leaves, I polled my friends, Mary, Ray, Michael and Carole, about whether I would be a good president and whether one of them would nominate me. They all said yes and Mary said she would nominate me. Then, we wondered who else might decide to run.

Bounding two steps at a time, I ran up the stairs to our apartment to tell Mom about my plans. On hearing the news, she revved her engines. Mom's idea of a class election was something akin to a Mickey Rooney–Judy Garland movie. Mom also possessed a savant's ability to rhyme and write jingles and I immediately began inventing snappy slogans. She even had an idea for a poster.

"We'll go to Kroch's and Brentano's and get supplies—confetti and streamers."

Mom was always supportive of my school activities and had clever ideas. I loved her suggestion of confetti and streamers and imagined the stir it would make in the classroom. It would be a like a real convention. This could really amp up the enthusiasm for the election.

But I soon realized this was no Hollywood musical. While I plotted our strategy with my pals after school, I didn't anticipate what was ahead.

Finally, the day of the nominations arrived. As we planned, Mary rose when Sister Bernard asked for nominations.

"I nominate Anita Solick for class president."

Now, our class was composed of 62 boys and three girls. The pubescent boys were like live wires and it took incredible energy to get their attention, much less educate them. Several of them had been held back, and some came from very disadvantaged families. Some did not speak English. Sister Bernard had her hands full.

Before Mary sat down, some boys hooted and yelled. Sister Bernard seemed to hesitate, but she regained her composure and asked for a second. Ray seconded the nomination. The class then voted on the nominees. When the votes were tallied, basketball captain Jim Miller and his popular and pretty girlfriend, Moe Sullivan, were on one ticket and Anita Solick and Daniel Ness were the other. I was ecstatic and ran home to tell Mom and the rest of the family...

But the next day when I returned to school, I got a rude awakening. This wasn't going to be so easy after all. Sister Bernard pulled me out of class and into the hall. She looked sheepish.

"Um, uh, I have some bad news."

"I am going to have to ask you to step down and accept the vice presidential slot and let Daniel run as president."

"What! Why?"

"Because, never in the history of St. Mel's has a girl ever run for class president."

My face reddened. I clenched my fists to avoid biting my nails. My ears got hot. I was livid. I couldn't believe what I was hearing. How unfair! Was she a woman or not? How could she ask me to do this? Maybe she liked being a second class citizen, but I was not one of them.

I sputtered. "Well, it's time one did—I won't step down, Sister."

Accustomed to compliant Catholic school girls, it took a minute for my surly response to register. She looked surprised and frowned. She repeated her request, but I stood firm.

"No, I won't step down—I won the nomination."

Sister was bewildered at my obstinacy, but she did not really know how stubborn I was. Speechless at my defiance, she motioned to me to return to class. I seethed through the catechism, science, and history lessons. When the bell rang, I stormed out.

My friends chased after me and surrounded me.

"Are you in trouble?"

"Probably. No—can you imagine the nerve? She wants me to step down because I am a girl."

"What did you say to her?"

"NO, of course!"

"Oooh!"

My pals commiserated with me about how unfair it was and how I would be the best class president ever. I thought Sister B openly favored the boys; she was a boy in a nun's habit. I knew she loved playing basketball with them every day, but I did not anticipate overt discrimination. I expected I'd have to run a great campaign against Jim and Moe. That did not deter me. I thought I had a good shot at it. Jim and Moe would run on their popularity. That would be hard to beat but I would take on the issues. I thought I could convince my classmates I was the best candidate and could beat them. I knew my running mate, Daniel, really wanted to run as president so I did not count on him for much help, but I thought he could pull in some of the boys' votes. So it was up to me.

When I arrived home from school, I poured out my frustration about my conversation with Sister Bernard to my mother. Mom was always a sympathizer, especially when it came to a righteous cause. Although Mom was a devout Catholic, there was a rebel in her, and she often encouraged us to question authority.

"I hope you told her no."

"I did—I think she was mad, but I stood up to her."

"Good, that's right; she can't tell you can't run. You won that nomination fair and square."

I thought the whole matter was closed, but when I got to school the next day, I was called to the principal's office for a talk. Sister Veronica Ann did not crack a smile as I entered her office on the mezzanine between the first and second floors of the school. She showed the little boy clutching his absence excuse out of her office with a dismissive wave.

I was still deluded that the nuns might support my feminist cause, and come over to my side, but I was quickly cured of my naiveté.

"Now, what's this business about you refusing to let Daniel run as president? That is not very charitable of you, Miss Solick, and pride is a sin. Do you think you are better than everyone else?"

I thought this was a particularly stupid question since obviously I did think I was better than everyone else or I wouldn't be running for office, but I decided it was wise not to respond. She was not satisfied with my silence and repeated the question.

"Well, Sister, yes, I am better qualified to run a campaign and to lead the class as President. I volunteered for Kennedy, remember?"

I gave her the quick rundown of my qualifications: top in the class, variety show star, etc. and, of course, experienced campaign volunteer. She was nonplussed and her expression did not change at all.

"You forgot one thing. You should have more humility, young woman and support your classmate with your campaign experience."

"Well, why should I—"

Sister cut me off.

"In the history of this school, there is no precedent for a girl running for class President of the 8th grade class. You must step down."

I knew I had to take a stand, even if it meant I would be at odds with the entire school administration. There was a lot at stake for me. I might jeopardize my class standing, scholarships, awards, who knew what else. But I stood firm. Anticipating her objections, I held my trump card to the last.

"Sister, I can't step down. My mother won't let me and I cannot disobey my mother. I have to run as President."

Sister Veronica Ann knew I had her with this argument. She did not want to tangle with my mom—the nun was too busy running an inner city school. She would just tell our pastor, the Bishop, that Helen Solick's child wouldn't yield. She ordered me to return to my classroom.

I threw my hands in the air in a gesture of triumph when I walked into Room 21. The girls clapped and some of the boys razzed me until Sister Bernard hushed them with the threat of demerits and a stay after school. Inside I was rejoicing. No one could tell me a girl wasn't good enough.

I ran home after school to tell Mom about my confrontation with Sister Veronica Ann. Shaking, I repeated my confrontation with the principal and my response. Mom grinned and approved.

"She has a lot of nerve. I'm glad you stood your ground. "

"But now you've got to get to work if you are going to win. Rome wasn't built in a day."

I wasn't planning on constructing a coliseum but I understood what she meant.

We got right to work on the campaign. Mom pulled out her rocket fuel—Cokes and bags of M&M's. She lit a cigarette and began free associations about election themes. I came up with "Solick for St. Mel's." Mom and I brainstormed our ideas for winning the Presidency for hours that evening at the big walnut dining room table. The posters, glitter, tempera paints, and markers purchased at Kroch's and Brentano's covered the whole surface. My sister, Barb, was recruited as my Creative Director and she set to work illustrating clever campaign posters. "Bright Ideas" was my campaign slogan. Barb worked up a big light bulb on the poster board, carefully hand lettering the main platform positions.

She even came up with one for my running mate, "Ness will clean up the mess" and created a poster with a spilled garbage can. I am not sure what the mess was, but Ness was going to take care of it. Barb came up with another poster with a child looking out from a tunnel to a bright sun and Mom devised a new slogan, "We'll show you the light with Anita's bright ideas. My campaign promises covered the poster—"Student Teachers", "Regular Study Hall", "More Field Trips", "Community Service Days", "High School/College Prep", and "Career Counseling".

I knew my ideas were advanced. I wanted to encourage activities that prepared us for high school and beyond. I thought it might be a tough sell to the teachers who were already overwhelmed with an average of 65 kids in each classroom, but I innocently thought my classmates would like these ideas.

Humming the tune to Chattanooga Choo Choo, Mom spontaneously began shouting out lines for a campaign song; her snapping fingers seemed to spur her on.

"Watch us soar ahead; our goals are high."

"There's no limit to our aims it's do or die."

"We're the St. Mel Crusaders and we'll get the job done."

While Mom rhymed word after word I listened in awe and wondered why she did not write poetry. I wasn't so sure I needed a song just yet, but she was on a roll and I knew better than to interrupt.

This was just the beginning. Mom, Barb and I would huddle around the dining room table every evening, plotting and tweaking our strategy. Sometimes Mary Lennon and other supporters would join us. We were determined to keep the pressure and awareness up. We designed a classroom activity for every day. We had a spontaneous rally in the classroom and threw confetti and streamers;

sometimes I would just ask permission to address the class; another day we gathered a crowd with campaign cheers and songs. It was something new every day. Meanwhile, my opponents smiled and waited. It was looking like they wouldn't mount any campaign at all. I worried when I saw they did not seem at all worried.

The day of the election I woke up so nervous and excited. I'd dreamed about winning and giving an acceptance speech before the entire class. I hurried to dress and grabbed a bowl of Kellogg's Corn Flakes before grabbing Barb and heading to school. Along the way we saw a couple of the punkie boys from my class.

"Hey, Solick, our man, Jim, is going to beat you. It's in the bag."

"I doubt it."

Barb and I turned our noses up at them and continued west on Madison Street towards St. Mel's School. But I had a strange premonition—how could they be so sure Jim would win? He hadn't done much to advance his candidacy. Did he know something I didn't know? I tried to shake off my apprehension; I didn't want my sister to see I was worried. When we got to school, we hugged. She wished me luck. I flashed her a thumbs-up and told her if I won it was because of her, and if I didn't, it was because of me. Then we headed to our respective classrooms.

The election was proving too exciting for my adolescent male classmates, and Sister Bernard could barely keep order. Boys were hopping out of their seats like frogs, talking aloud in class, throwing notes to their buddies, and shooting spitballs. It was pandemonium. Sister gave each candidate the floor for a few minutes to make their final pitch before the voting began. I'd prepared a speech that succinctly covered my platform. My opponent stood briefly.

"Vote for me. I am the basketball captain."

He sat down. That's it? That's all you got? Well, I am voting for me, and so should everyone else.

Sister explained the voting procedures again. The four classes would be allowed to cast their votes for President and Vice President. The teachers for all grades could also cast their votes. Proctors were designated to collect the votes from the teachers and the other classrooms and bring them to Room 21. Sister would count all the ballots and after the voting was finished and the ballots counted, the winner would be announced.

The sickly sweet smelling mimeographed ballots had been distributed a few days before, so naturally some kids either forgot or lost them and needed replacement ballots. Students had to identify themselves if they'd lost their ballot and get a new one, along with a chiding from Sister Bernard. This took a few minutes. Then Sister instructed the class to mark the ballot with their choice and when they were ready to bring it up to her desk. This went on for what seemed like a year to this impatient candidate. I couldn't believe some kids waited until today to make a decision. Sister Bernard wanted quiet and we were instructed to select a story from Lives of the Saints and read silently until everyone finished voting. Periodically, there would be a knock at the classroom door, and a child would appear with ballots from another classroom or another teacher.

Several hours passed and then Sister grew impatient and announced that the students had five more minutes to make a decision. But, I worried; did the other classrooms know she was closing the polls? She instructed the students to pass any remaining ballots forward. She counted the few remaining ballots and looked up. There was a knock on the door. Two children came in with ballots in hand, but Sister declared that the voting was closed and these ballots were disqualified. One girl interrupted Sister. I thought I saw a tear in her eye.

"But these kids were sick. Their moms brought the ballots to the principal's office and she told us to bring them up here when we were delivering messages to the classrooms."

The other girl told Sister that she'd picked up the ballots from teachers on her rounds delivering supplies and brought them up when she finished her rounds. She said she did not know that the voting would close or she would have brought them first thing. But Sister shook her head.

"I declared the voting closed. We have a winner."

I blurted out, "Sister, who are those votes for?"

She replied that she wouldn't tell us because they were disqualified and she'd declared the voting closed. I felt sure they were for me. Otherwise, why not tell?

My heart sank.

"The winners are Jim Miller and Maureen Sullivan."

I felt the election was rigged and I'd lost.

Hypocrites!

I was furious, not just for myself, but for Mom and Barb, and my friends who'd worked in earnest to get me elected.

Then I had a moment of realization—this was what I'd face for the rest of my life. I would have to fight against the status quo, and wouldn't always win. Sometimes the people I expected to be on my side wouldn't be. It was so unfair; I was disillusioned, and, in that moment, the authority figures at my school lost all credibility with me. I was finished—it was over. I would move on. I made a decision right then and vowed I would apply for high schools outside of my neighborhood. And I vowed to continue my fight against injustice.

Barb and I walked home a lot slower that day, dragging our saddle shoes, not wanting to tell Mom the results, not wanting to disappoint her. She'd put so much energy into this. I tried to think how I would break the news to her, but I didn't have to tell her. When she opened the front door and saw the sad look on my face she knew the results.

"They cheated me. Sister disqualified some of the votes and Jim Miller won."

I knew this wouldn't go down well with Mom; she was like a tigress when someone bothered her children. Mom flipped. Her face got redder and redder as she pressed me for the details. She lit and abandoned one cigarette after another.

"How dare they? After we donated to their damned building fund? I ought to cancel the pledge. We'll never use that hall anyway. And, then, the ultimate threat—"I'm going up there."

Almost true to her word, Mom called the school and made a stink, but the principal wouldn't allow her to challenge her authority in their school and wouldn't reverse the decision.

Always the pragmatist, Mom advised me to forget it.

"You're not getting a paycheck for being class president. Find something else to win. "

I knew she was right and decided to take her advice. I did not win that election but there were other personal triumphs. I won the class debates and the science fair. The recruiters from a new high school came to our class and talked about how the new students would be in the first graduating class. I got the paperwork from the recruiter and filled out my application. I entered a Chicago-wide writing contest and won. I decided to embrace my role as a trailblazer.

Two years later, I was a high school girl in a rolled up uniform skirt who wore dark eye makeup and was crazy for the Beatles. I'd forgotten all about the election; it seemed like a million years ago. Then, inspired by my example, one of Barb's girlfriends ran for class president and won. Barb was her campaign manager and she incorporated the techniques we pioneered in my unsuccessful campaign to secure a win for her friend.

While working on an assignment for journalism class, Barb burst in and, flush with success, announced their victory.

"We did it. Ellen won!"

I felt like it was a triumph for me and for every girl. The male tradition was broken. Other girls would run for president and win. Other girls would break down barriers and win and win again.

Years later, when the former Sister Bernard and I became Facebook friends and exchanged emails, she expressed her regret that I hadn't won that election. Comparing me to Hillary Clinton, she wrote, "And, I guess, the world still isn't ready for a woman president." I knew she was wrong.

Epilogue

Moving day. The living room was empty except for one item. I kicked at the corner of the rose colored oriental rug with my high school uniform saddle shoe. The once beautiful rose-colored rug, moth eaten and damaged from Aunt Marie's dogs on one end, had covered our living room floor for years. Mom always said she would send it to be repaired and even got a quote, but never followed through. We'd danced and played and dreamed on that rug. Now, our family was starting a new chapter.

The rug was given to my great grandfather during the depression as settlement of a debt for a wedding reception held at Solick's Restaurant. Possession of the rug was the origin of a family rift—a rift that exposed old wounds, past injustices, anger that had festered for generations. The rug became a symbol and was start of a family feud that would result in our move from our beloved Madison Street.

We were heading to the Northwest Side of Chicago. Bantam Books, Dad's second job, had moved from down by the Chicago River to Des Plaines. Mom wanted me to attend a new school, Mother Guerin High School, administered by her cherished Sisters of Providence. I'd been commuting on the CTA to River Grove for a year. Dad was transferred to a new firehouse. Moving made sense.

And neither Dad nor his sister, Mary, wanted anything to do with the restaurant. In the end, an argument over the old rug, which Aunt Marie gave to us and then tried to repossess after it was cleaned, doomed Solick's Restaurant. The corporation was dissolved, and all assets were liquidated. We left—never to return to the West Side.

Some years later, Dad heard there had been a fire at the old restaurant. He rushed to the scene to see if the stained-glass doors with the capital S that his grandfather had imported from Bohemia could be saved, but a salvage firm had scraped the building. Nothing remained. It is still a vacant lot today.

And the oriental rug? It was too large for any room in our Chicago bungalow on New England. Mom relegated it to the unfinished basement, and tossed it a few years later when flooding further damaged it. We moved on.

About the Author

Anita Solick Oswald is a Chicago native. She's written a collection of essays, West Side Girl that chronicle the colorful, diverse and oftentimes unpredictably eccentric characters and events that populated Chicago's West Side neighborhood during the 50's & 60's. Her essays have appeared in The Write Place at the Write Time, the Faircloth Literary Review, The Fat City Review, and Avalon Literary Review.

Anita grew up in the 3rd story apartment above her family's Bohemian restaurant on Madison Street, daughter of a fireman and a housewife/frustrated writer, and comrade of a ragtag brigade of migrant children who trooped into and found both themselves and the world-at-large on their neighborhood's streets.

Anita studied journalism at Marquette University, earned her B.A. in Economics from the University of California at Los Angeles and her M.S. in Management from the University of Colorado. She lives in Niwot, Colorado, with her husband, Ralph, and her cats, Ziggy and Clio. Anita's daughters, Deirdre and Barbara, and grandson, Declan, live nearby.